Embroidery
& Nature

Embroidery & Nature

Jan Messent

B T Batsford Ltd   London

Acknowledgment

This book would never have been produced without the encouragement and help of Thelma Nye, to whom I owe sincere thanks. My thanks also go to Valerie Harding for her advice and help in taking so many of the excellent photographs for me, to Jan Beaney and her City and Guilds students at the Maidenhead and Windsor College of Further Education, and other friends and acquaintances who have generously allowed me to use their embroideries and drawings. To Gail Bathgate and Roger Cuthbert I extend my thanks for photographing work so beautifully, involving many feats of organisation. To my family, thank you for again suffering the organised chaos of 'bookmaking' and embroidery, and for your loving help and co-operation at all times.

Cover photograph: 'Lichen and Fungi' by Barbara Snook: crewel wool and stranded cotton yarns on soft brown woollen hopsack (photograph by John Hunnex)

© Jan Messent 1980
First published 1980
Reprinted 1981
First published in paperback 1983

ISBN 0 7134 1832 X

Filmset in Monophoto Sabon
by Servis Filmsetting Ltd,
Manchester

Printed by The Anchor Press,
Tiptree, Essex

for the publishers B T Batsford Ltd
4 Fitzhardinge Street, London
W1H 0AH

Contents

Frontispiece: 'A Tree for All Seasons' by
Jackey Hill (photograph by R.H. Cuthbert)

Introduction

This is a book of ideas for embroiderers, many of whom, although aware of some of the design material available to them from the world of nature, would welcome an inducement to explore it further.

The portrayal of all aspects of nature has been universally popular with embroiderers for thousands of years. We know this from the remnants of fabrics found in burial places as far apart as Russia, Egypt and South America. These show birds, hares, horses, wild and mythological animals, with borders and geometrical shapes containing foliage of all kinds. Nearer our own time, in the early middle ages, plant and animal forms were often enclosed within roundels and rectangles, embroidered on church vestments and heraldic banners belonging to noble families and guilds. There are very few countries which have never made use of natural forms in their traditional embroidery.

Nature has been portrayed in such textile crafts as lace, weaving, knitting, crochet, and carpet and rug making as well as in embroidery in a wide variety of materials. In China and Japan exquisite garments are worked in sumptuous gold thread and pure silk on satin. In 15th century South America, mythological creatures were woven and embroidered in handspun llama and vicuna hair. More recently, the first settlers in North America made cotton patchwork quilts depicting flowers and animals among the motifs, while the American Indians portrayed stylised lightning, buffalo and wild flowers in materials such as wool, cotton, beads, porcupine quills and moose hair. Glass, leather, feathers and paint all play their part in embroidery while the tool box of a professional embroiderer today would raise many an eyebrow.

The styles of design used in various countries are even more numerous than the materials with which they are worked. Compare the rigid cross-stitch foliage seen in some peasant work of Europe, the highly complicated swirling designs of Japan and China, the formal chain stitch figures on the ancient Peruvian burial shrouds and the child-like simplicity of English Elizabethan insects and flowers. Each country has its own unique and recognisable styles in embroidery, that used at the present time as well as those which have passed into history.

With this great diversity of material before us, not only from our own countries but those belonging to others, to other civilisations, in other materials and styles, what can *we* find in nature to draw upon for our own ideas? Has it all been said, even better than we could say it? The answer to this must be that there are no really 'new' ways of doing things, only old ways done differently, but because of the combination of materials, technique and purpose to be taken into consideration, as well as the wider ones of tradition, country, fashion, personal experience and skill, there will always be someone, somewhere, finding a different approach to the subject.

Every embroidery designer, whether just beginning or more experienced, can be helped to find that different way by learning to look at nature in a more perceptive way than has perhaps been the case. It is well known that no two people ever produce a piece of work exactly the same – though some may try. With that comforting thought to spur us on in our efforts to be unique, it is hoped that the suggestions which follow will be of some value.

1 This dog (*above*) from the Bayeaux Tapestry appears in a similar position to the one on a mola (*right*) made by Cuna Indians of the San Blas Islands, Panama

7

2 Chilcat sleeveless jumper made by North American Indians of the Pacific coast, showing abstract bears and monsters (courtesy of Pitt Rivers Museum, University of Oxford)

3 *Right* Hanging from a Buddhist Temple at Chien-in, Kyoto, Japan, worked in coloured silks and gold thread on black canvas covered with paper, mainly in long and short stitch (Crown copyright, courtesy of the Victoria and Albert Museum)

4 (a) Design from a 17th century
English pattern book by Peter Stent,
now in the British Museum
(b) Border design from a long pillow
cover, English, 16th century
(c and d) Butterfly and snail from
English embroideries of the late 16th
and early 17th centuries; they
decorated samplers, long covers,
sleeve panels, and were transferred
from pattern books onto the fabric
ready for embroidery in the chosen
colour
(e) Tree from the Bradford Table
Carpet, worked in tent stitch on
canvas, English, 17th century

5 (a and b) Leaf motifs from early American patchwork quilts
(c, d and e) Animal motifs from woven textiles of 11th century Peru
(f) Naturalistic designs from a beaded bandolier bag of Chippewa, Wisconsin

6 Embroidered fragment from the Island of Skyros, Greece, probably part of a bed hanging; the exotic bird, thought to be a woodcock, is embroidered in double darning in red, blue, yellow, apricot, green, black and white threads on natural linen (courtesy of the Embroiderers' Guild, London)

7 *Far right* Japanese embroidery of the 18th to 19th centuries from Fukusa; the birds are probably cranes, worked in gold thread and coloured silks on dark satin (Crown copyright, courtesy of the Victoria and Albert Museum)

Research

Time taken to do preliminary research into a subject before designing is *essential* and will repay the student a hundredfold in terms of time saved, familiarity with all aspects of the chosen subject and suitability for the technique in mind.

This may be awkward when the subject – perhaps a beautiful view seen quickly through a car window – cannot be studied in detail, yet the only thing in one's mind from then on is to create it instantly in fabric and thread. Unless one is a fairly experienced designer, this will come under the heading of 'experiments' because, although a valid and spontaneous piece of work, it will also be a 'hit or miss' one.

There is much the student can do individually long before taking work to a class or turning to anyone else for advice. Here are some ways of researching a subject which will help to make designing pleasanter, smoother and more interesting.

1   Gather together as much information as possible about the subject from cuttings, postcards, sketches and photographs. These should help to supply details of shapes, colours, textures, patterns, environment and so on. Libraries are a great help in this.

2   Obtain photostats of material not belonging to you and keep these for reference. Make a note of where each piece of information was obtained; this will ensure that it can be found again if necessary.

3   Draw and photograph the subject many times, at different times of the day and in different weather conditions if it is out of doors. Draw it from all angles. (Do not be afraid to draw; it is a skill which, like being able to write, can be learnt by anyone. Practice and persistence will have a remarkable effect on results in a very short time. If you feel intimidated by white paper, use a soft pencil or fibre pen on coloured paper, or pen and ink, charcoal, paint or pastel.)

4   Keep all your references together neatly in a scrapbook or on a display card with any relevant notes. Arrange them with swatches of threads and fabrics showing colours and textures.

5   Try out details of your subject in embroidery techniques. If you are unfamiliar with a technique you wish to use, obtain books from the library and learn something about it. Work part of a leaf or flower, for instance, in quilting, appliqué, blackwork or canvaswork. This will help to discover the limitations of both the design and the technique and allow you to adjust one to suit the other.

6   Visit craft exhibitions showing textiles, ceramics, woodwork, metalwork, jewellery and embroidery. Seeing other people's work often helps the designer with such things as proportion, balance, colour, materials, subject matter and technique.

7   Design sources can also be found in textile designs of other countries, both woven and embroidered. The study of peasant embroidery and samplers will reveal enchanting designs from nature which can easily be adapted for a simple border design in cross stitch, canvas embroidery, Assisi work, blackwork, pulled thread or cutwork.

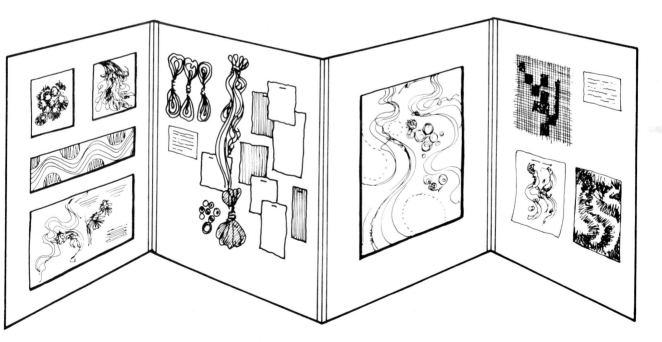

8 Reference notes may be kept on a card like this which will fold away when not in use; here you can see at a glance all the material you have acquired

16

9 *Left* Pencil drawings of plants by Judith Milne, exploring the structure from various angles, with some shown in detail

10 *Below left* A detail of canvaswork by Evelyn Griffiths exploring the directions made by various stitches (photograph by David Prout)

11 *Below right* Peasant embroideries suggest delightful designs of plant life: the small one is from an early 16th century German sampler, and the tree is a woven design from Sweden, made in 1781, symbolising life

12 (a) There are many ways in which an area of foliage like this could be translated into embroidery: a three-dimensional approach may be tried, or perhaps stitchery (photograph by R H Cuthbert)
(b) Try out some stitches which give the same effect as that made by the grass and leaves; those shown here are cretan, buttonhole, Portuguese knotted stem, detached chain and french knots (photograph by R H Cuthbert)

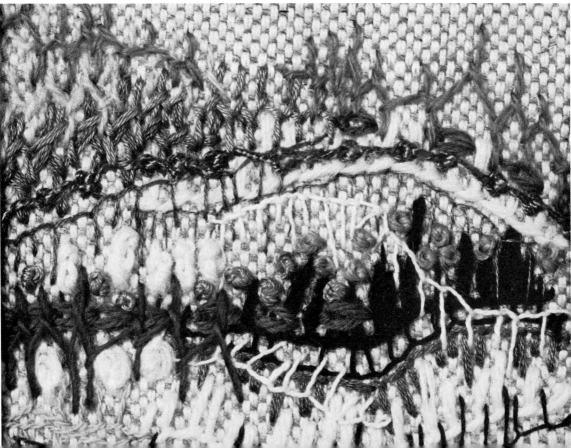

13 *Right* The decorative grain on this little wooden bull may suggest lines of stitchery or quilting; ideas from nature worked in other media are often a rich source of inspiration

14 Page of research material by Heide Jenkins, showing feathers, feather patterns, tie-dyed patchwork, feather shapes and a drawing showing its possible use on a garment (photograph by V A Harding)

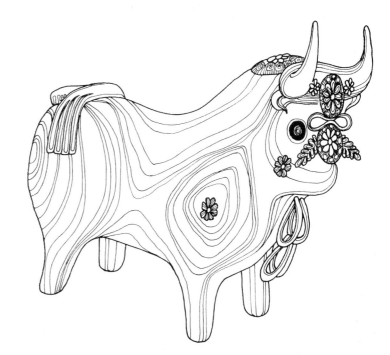

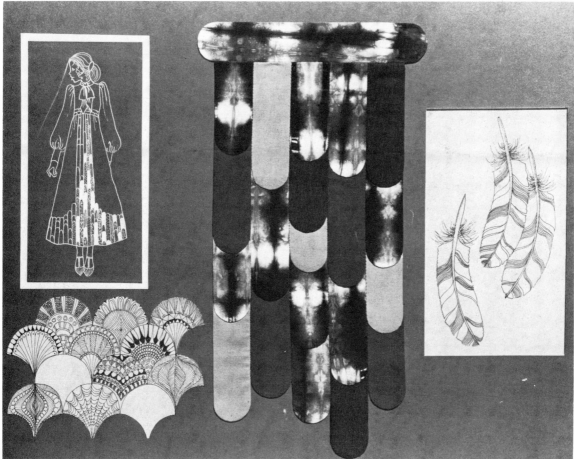

Experiments

Once the research has been well established, experiments in design can begin. Do not be tempted to make your experiments into functional objects; they will be more useful to you if they are mounted or filed away with their relevant research notes for use as reference material prior to beginning your embroidery. The following suggestions may help you to use the research material you have gathered and translate it into design.

Two important points to note before commencing are: (a) always try to work in a good light and with enough space, and (b) try to obtain conditions conducive to quiet thought and concentration. This is sometimes difficult in busy households, but can often be arranged with careful planning.

1 A drawing or photograph may be very interesting in one particular area which can be isolated from the rest by cutting two pieces of card to form right-angled corners. These are then placed over the drawing or photograph with the area of interest framed inside them. They can be moved about until the best arrangement is found.

2 Cut a drawing or photograph up into squares or strips and rearrange them to form a pattern or an abstract design.

3 Children's books, garden catalogues and advertisements are good sources of ideas. In recent years they have become more exciting than ever, providing a wealth of imaginative treatments and colours. Carefully trace over a clear photograph of a flower and try various ways of outlining the petals.

4 From your own flower drawing, try a series of experiments to isolate the whole plant shape without any details, first with, and then without shaded parts. Place only parts of it inside a frame.

5 Designing with cut paper lends itself well to those techniques which require shapes to be filled in, rather than lines. These would include blackwork, canvaswork, padded quilting, appliqué and pulled work. It is also particularly suited to those people who prefer to cut out shapes with scissors rather than draw with a pencil. Different kinds of paper, newsprint, brown wrapping paper, tissue, cartridge and magazine pages will help to organise tonal areas.

6   Similarly, torn paper designing is very effective when used to create outdoor scenes involving areas of land, hills, trees and other foliage. For this, *tear* shapes out of the papers mentioned above and arrange them as areas of scenery. The rough edges often seem to be more realistic than cut paper. The pieces may overlap at any point, and can be fixed with glue. Use a paper frame to establish the border of your finished design.

7   To build a design from geometric shapes, lay a piece of tracing paper over a picture (of an animal, for instance) and draw in shapes to cover the animal's body, taking care to observe the natural joints, shadows and creases. These will help to determine the size and arrangement of the shapes.

8   Use string, seeds, metal washers and other small objects to build up a design in the form of a collage. These may be stuck down with glue onto a firm paper, either self-coloured or patterned. Lines of closely-laid string helps to design for corded quilting.

9   Designs may sometimes arise quite accidentally from 'doodles' which may suggest embroidery. Use letters of the alphabet, numbers, punctuation marks and other symbols to build a shape. There are no rules; letters may be repeated, of different sizes, or perhaps those making up a name. Use this idea for appliqué on children's clothes, bags, belts, quilts and novelty cushions.

10   Draw curved lines across a drawing of a flower, tree, fish or animal to divide it up into a patchwork design. Undulating lines, when drawn across a moving animal, help to create an effect of rippling muscles, camouflage and rhythm.

11   Shapes within a design will often overlap each other. This can sometimes be dealt with by using a darker tone on some of the shapes, or by making some solid and others linear. Some shapes could also be padded to make them stand away from the background and others worked in corded quilting.

12   An abstract design can be made by laying tracing paper over a drawing or photograph and redrawing the darkest parts only, omitting all other shapes. If this results in a too-fragmented arrangement, block in those shapes which have the next darkest tonal value.

13   A drawing may be reduced to its simplest possible form to produce a symbol. This is particularly successful with flowers and some plants, trees, fish and other reasonably simple shapes in nature. The embroidery on the shepherd's smock is an example of this; the one in figure 28 symbolises woolly sheep inside hurdles with possibly the curling horns too.

14   A stylised interpretation requires the designer to choose the most important points of a subject and use them as the main elements in a carefully balanced and decorative manner. This is a particularly satisfactory style for use with stitchery, pulled work and metal thread embroidery as these sometimes call for a more controlled method of presenting stitches, threads and areas of pattern.

15   If the idea of portraying a complete outdoor scene is a little too daunting, try drawing a detail from it instead. Sketching outdoor scenes will be easier if a small area is selected for study, for example a clump of lush foliage or a beautiful tree trunk.

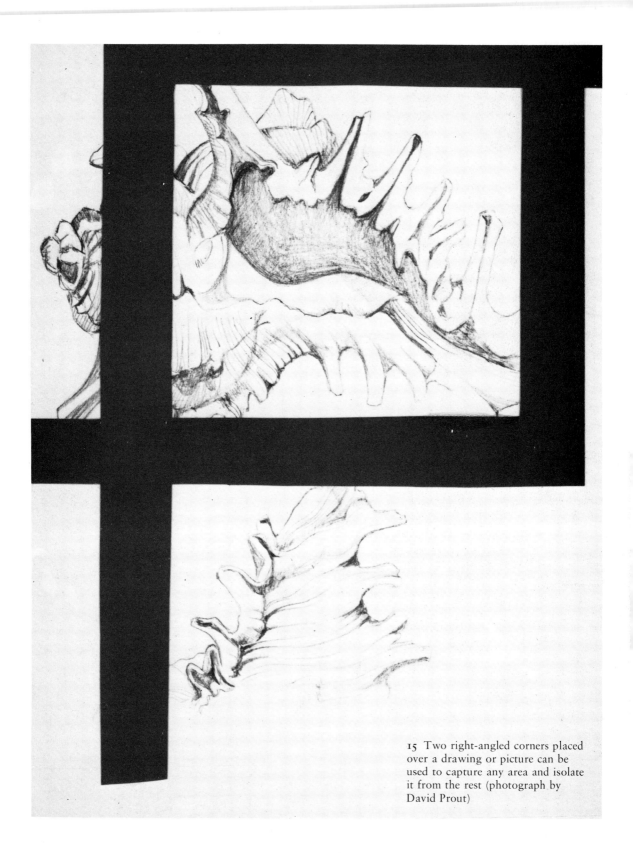

15 Two right-angled corners placed over a drawing or picture can be used to capture any area and isolate it from the rest (photograph by David Prout)

16 A drawing can be cut up into squares and rearranged

17 *Below left* A design from a children's book which would be simple to embroider

18 *Below right* This design was used in an advertisement and was made of sheet metal: the highly stylised contours make this horse perfect for embroidery

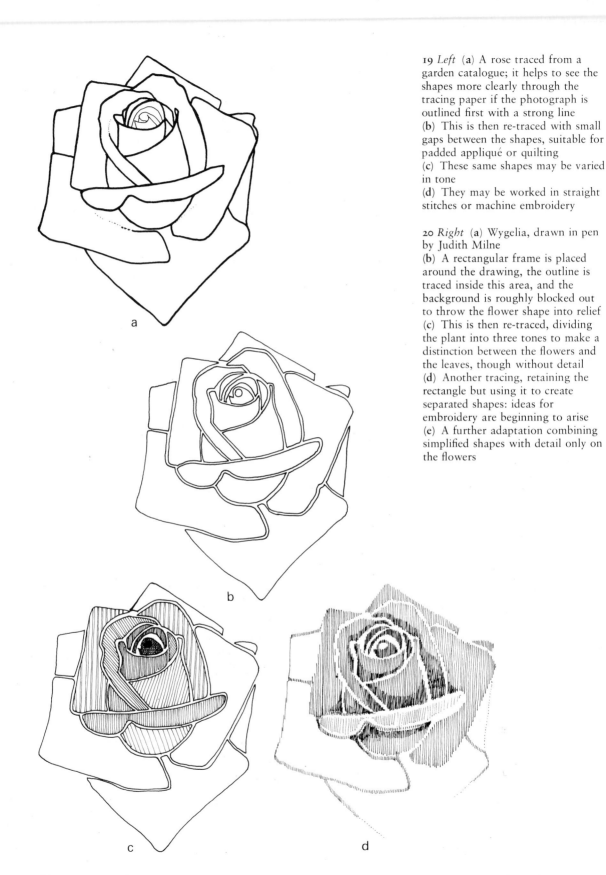

19 *Left* (a) A rose traced from a garden catalogue; it helps to see the shapes more clearly through the tracing paper if the photograph is outlined first with a strong line
(b) This is then re-traced with small gaps between the shapes, suitable for padded appliqué or quilting
(c) These same shapes may be varied in tone
(d) They may be worked in straight stitches or machine embroidery

20 *Right* (a) Wygelia, drawn in pen by Judith Milne
(b) A rectangular frame is placed around the drawing, the outline is traced inside this area, and the background is roughly blocked out to throw the flower shape into relief
(c) This is then re-traced, dividing the plant into three tones to make a distinction between the flowers and the leaves, though without detail
(d) Another tracing, retaining the rectangle but using it to create separated shapes: ideas for embroidery are beginning to arise
(e) A further adaptation combining simplified shapes with detail only on the flowers

a

b

c

d

hygelia

a

b

c

d

e

21 *Above* Shell design for blackwork
using various tones of paper
(photograph by David Prout)

22 Cat design based on geometric
shapes made by tracing over a
drawing or photograph

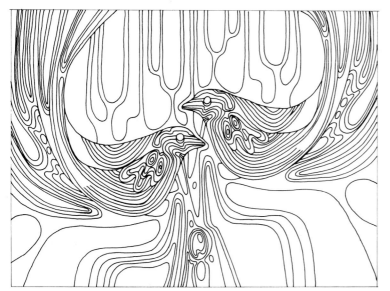

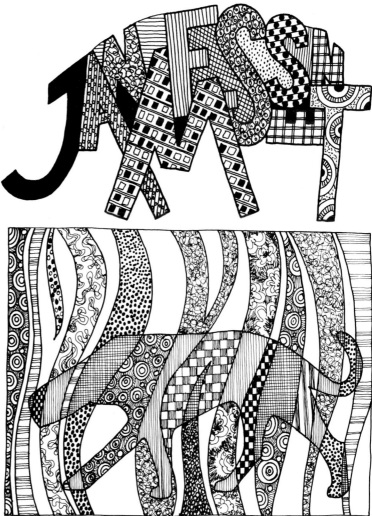

23 *Top* Lines of string glued onto card often suggest designs for corded quilting

24 *Centre* A 'doodle' back-to-front animal made up of the letters in the author's name

25 Curved lines drawn across a picture often suggest movement as well as creating an effective background

26 *Above* (a) A bunch of garlic makes an attractive subject for embroidery, either in quilting, appliqué, goldwork or stitchery

(b) Some shapes are made more obvious while others recede

27 A tracing was made from a drawing of a cactus, shading only the darkest areas, thus creating an abstract design (by Vera Bradshaw)

28 Shepherd's smock, showing the symbolic sheep hurdles and curling horns (courtesy of the Museum of English Rural Life, University of Reading, Berkshire)

29 Paint and pen sketch of an owl in a stylised manner suitable for padded appliqué and stitchery (photograph by Gail Bathgate)

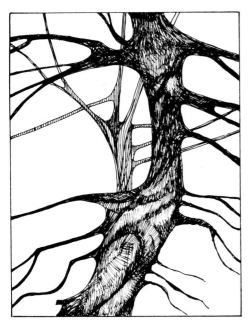

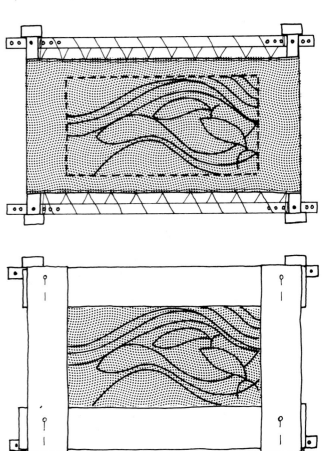

30 *Above left* Pen drawing of a section of a cedar of Lebanon tree; by eliminating the foliage the full beauty of the twisting trunk and branches is accentuated

31 *Left* Pencil drawing of a peperomia, by Judith Milne – notice the concentration of detail on the stem rather than the leaves; this method of recording helps to focus the attention on one part only, thus establishing areas of primary and secondary importance, which is a preliminary stage in designing

32 *Above right* Fix strips of paper round the worked area with pins to cover the excess material (see page 36)

This page and overleaf

33 Six experiments made by children during the Berkshire Branch Embroiderers' Guild exhibition of 1978; motifs were drawn onto small squares of calico which children were invited to embroider as they wished, and the pieces were then sewn together to make a 'Garden Patchwork' (photographs by R H Cuthbert)

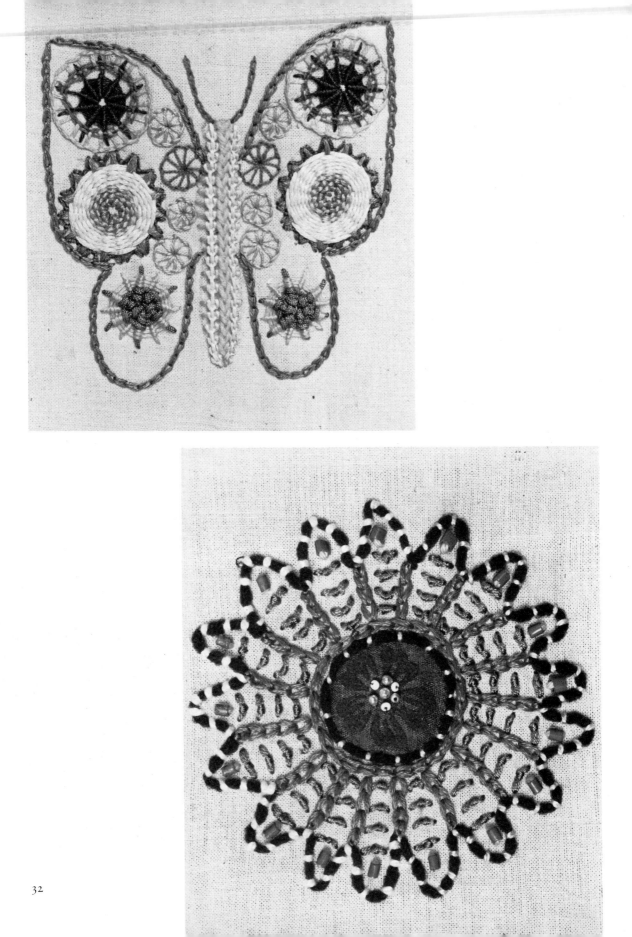

33 (Contd) Experiments made by children during the Berkshire Branch Embroiderers' Guild exhibition of 1978 (see page 31)

Space

Space in a design is necessary to give the eye room to travel round and then rest awhile before being led back to the most interesting part, the focal point. If the design is overcrowded and fussy, the eye will be led along too many paths in its search for something more satisfying, and eventually may give up altogether if the process proves too demanding.

Always be aware of the spaces between the shapes you have made, and of their relationships with each other. Give 'breathing space' to the busier areas of texture and pattern by *not* allowing unnecessary lines and shapes to crowd in wherever a space exists.

The Background

The background is as much a part of the design as the other parts and should therefore be seen and planned along with the rest of the design and not as an afterthought. Some ideas for its treatment are suggested here:

1   Use the same technique as that on the main subject, but on a different scale.

2   Use the same colour but choose a textural effect for the background which differs from that of the main subject.

3   Use the natural pattern of the subject on a smaller scale, e.g. a repeat pattern, spots, stripes, leaves or flowers.

4   Use shapes, colours and stitches which will help to camouflage an animal in its surroundings. The arctic fox, hare and owl, the ptarmigan and nightjar, the zebra and giraffe are creatures which camouflage well, so choose colours and techniques which accentuate this.

5   Use a patterned fabric to create a ready-made environment. Jungle-type prints, floral or abstract patterns can be used effectively in this way.

6   (a) Use fabric dyes to paint a design on the background fabric before embroidering on it.
(b) Tie-dye the fabric and use the resulting effect as part of the design.
(c) Use the batik (wax-resist) method of creating a textural effect on the background fabric.

7   Work lines of corded quilting under a plain fabric to suggest ripples of water, cliffs, trees, grasses, shadows and reflections.

8   Experiment with lines suggested by the bars of a cage, trees and foliage, nests, burrow systems and honeycomb.

Design Analysis

Embroiderers often reach a stage when they would welcome constructive criticism and advice about a piece of work which is not progressing satisfactorily. When advice is not available, try the following methods of analysis:

1 While the embroidery is still on the frame it is often difficult to tell how it will look when finished, so to eliminate the extra fabric round the edge, pin wide strips of plain paper around it as shown in figure 32. This will help to establish the position of the focal point.

2 Hold the design up in front of a mirror and see it in reverse. This helps to clarify points of imbalance or some other fault which was not obvious before.

3 Put the embroidery away for a time, several days if possible, with a cover over it. Then, when your mind is refreshed, take another look and you may soon see where the faults are.

4 Are you trying to force a design and technique to work together which are incompatible? Is there another technique which would have expressed the subject better?

Nature in Colour

Nature offers an endless variety of colour schemes from which the embroiderer may draw inspiration, and to experiment with them is probably one of the most exciting and rewarding experiences in designing. No amount of theory can help as much as the observation and study of nature's colour changes from one season to the next. This is particularly so in countries where the weather and seasons play an important part in the lives of its people.

Our own gardens, however large or small, reflect colour changes almost hourly, even in the long grass which is then mowed to a paler tone, passes from sunshine to cloud, then into evening sunset and darkness. Experiment by recording the changing tones and colours of one scene from first light to darkness, or in a series starting with Spring going through to Winter. Record the colours of a pet animal in these changing conditions, a shell on the window-sill or a tree in its various stages of undress.

Autumn
by Katy Bartlett

Come Autumn, Robinia Frisia * is taken unawares.
She still wears her light bright golden dress made for garden
   parties.
October's first damp misty entrance leaves her wearing a gown of
   drab sour yellow.
Frail and frosty cobwebs cling to her bare twigs
Dampened afresh with every new morn.
The sun tries to spruce up her fading finery.
Briefly, she is dappled with golden sunlight – but all in vain.
For Winter, she has nothing to wear.

(*Mock Acacia)

Experiment freely with colours seen in a butterfly's wing, a cat's fur, a plant with variegated leaves such as the coleus, a patch of lichen or a piece of mineral. Look closely at a kipper, or any other fish to see what colours are there and record them in paint or in any other medium.

Gather together any fabrics, wools and other threads, paper, leaves, feathers, etc. of the colours you find in your chosen subject, together with paint sketches, drawings and notes, and keep these together for reference. Fleeting observations made out of doors may be scribbled down – with comments like 'blue-brownish grey here' or 'bronze tones with black spots' if there is no other way to record them at the time.

Remember that you are *designing*, therefore you may exaggerate or play down any colours you wish in order to obtain the desired effect and fulfil the purpose of the embroidery.

Subjects to study
Observe and record the following

1   *Changing times of day*
    early morning, noon, dusk, moonlight.

2   *Changing weather*
    dull, misty, bright sunshine, rain, snow, frost, storm.

3   *Changing seasons*
    Spring – pale greens, yellow, blue, white, pink.

    Summer – brilliant greens (all tones), red, yellow, blue (primary colours), hard shadows and contrasts.

    Autumn – gold, mellow yellows, brown/grey/beige, russet, red, softening colours.

    Winter – white, silver, grey/blue, mauve, grey/browns, muted colours.

4   *Changing life*
    birth to death cycle of insects and plants, e.g.
    (i) fruit: immature, ripe, decaying;
    (ii) fern: unfolding, mature, dying;
    (iii) butterfly: caterpillar, chrysalis, imago.

5   *Changing seashore*
    colour of the tides, sand and rocks, seaweed, reflections and ripples.

6   *Changing landscapes*
    varying soil colours, brown, grey, white, buff. Distance mutes colour, often adds blue/mauve. Clouds make patches of shadow. Patchwork fields – greens, yellows, brown, black (burnt stubble), mauve (heather).

7   *Flowers*
    gardening catalogues, flower and gardening shops.

8   *Animals*
    hamsters, cats, rabbits, exotic birds in zoos and museums.

9   Underwater life: coral, weeds, shells, fish, rocks and minerals.

34 Some of the aspects of nature from which one may draw ideas for colour schemes: look closely at ordinary things like mossy stones and pieces of seaweed – it is likely that what appears at first to be one colour may prove to be a mixture of many

35 A section of Mexican lace agate, showing a wonderful array of pinks, red, brown, grey and white (photograph by Norman Weston)

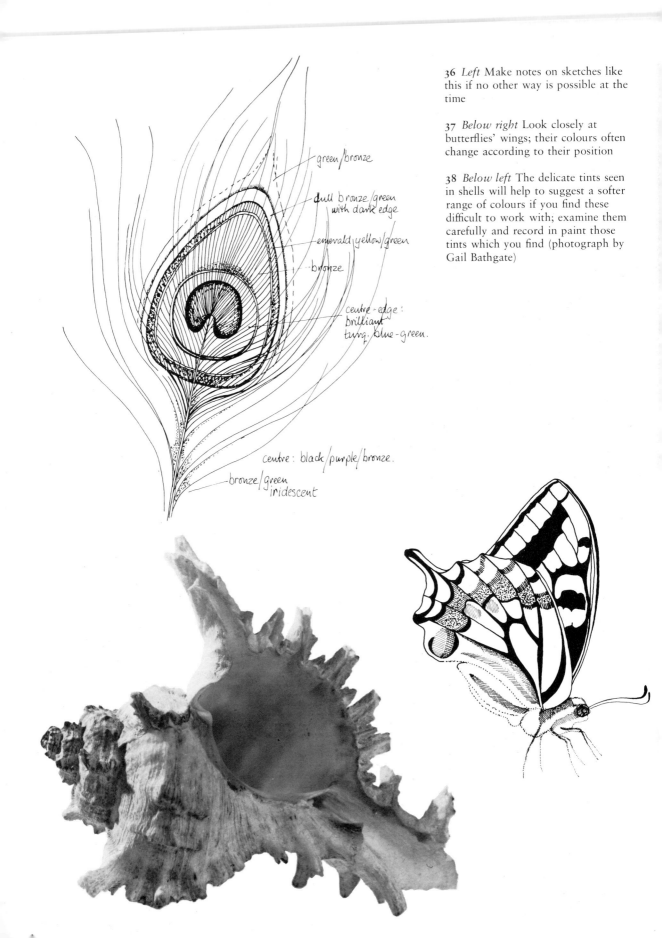

green/bronze

dull bronze/green
with dark edge

emerald/yellow/green

bronze

centre-edge:
brilliant
turq. blue-green.

centre: black/purple/bronze.

bronze/green
iridescent

36 *Left* Make notes on sketches like this if no other way is possible at the time

37 *Below right* Look closely at butterflies' wings; their colours often change according to their position

38 *Below left* The delicate tints seen in shells will help to suggest a softer range of colours if you find these difficult to work with; examine them carefully and record in paint those tints which you find (photograph by Gail Bathgate)

39 The flowers in one's garden or window box provide a wealth of colours from which to choose: note the various shades of green in different types of plants (photograph by Judith Milne)

40 (a) Animals vary greatly in their markings, usually ranging through tones of one colour; break down the areas of colour to form a series of interlocking shapes
(b) The design can be further simplified and used as the basis of a multicoloured appliqué panel, or the pattern for a hooked rug worked on canvas

41 Fish are a particularly rich source of ideas for colour: study a golden kipper and note its shimmering scales and blue-grey patches against the bronze

a

b

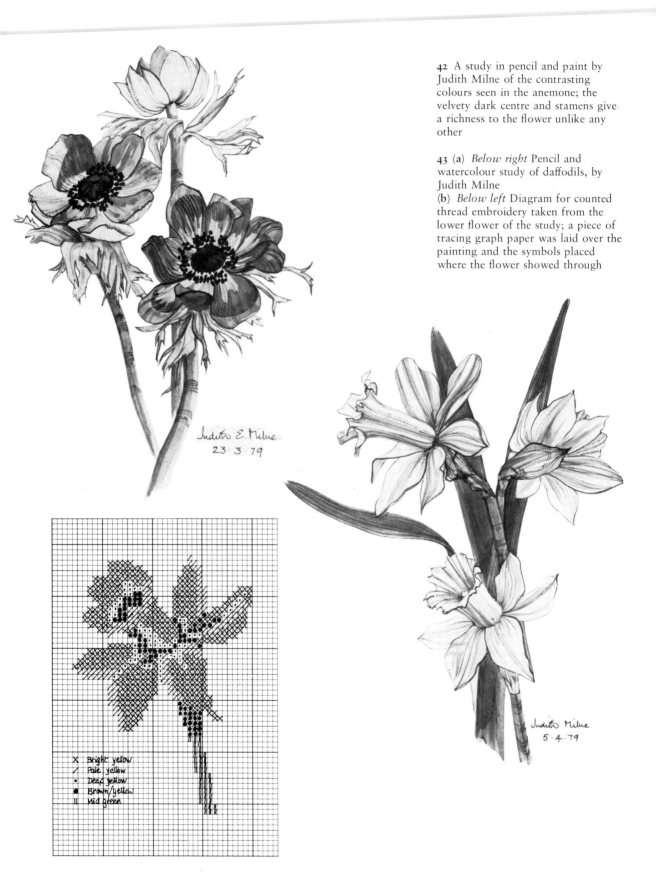

42 A study in pencil and paint by Judith Milne of the contrasting colours seen in the anemone; the velvety dark centre and stamens give a richness to the flower unlike any other

43 (a) *Below right* Pencil and watercolour study of daffodils, by Judith Milne
(b) *Below left* Diagram for counted thread embroidery taken from the lower flower of the study; a piece of tracing graph paper was laid over the painting and the symbols placed where the flower showed through

Judith E. Milne.
23.3.79

X Bright yellow
/ Pale yellow
• Deep yellow
● Brown/yellow
‖ Mid green

Judith Milne
5.4.79

44 (a) 'A Tree for all Seasons' by
Jackey Hill; this side shows the
blossoms of Spring turning into the
fruits of Summer (photograph by
R H Cuthbert)
(b) This side shows the leaves of
Summer turning into the brown
skeletons of Autumn, which are then
tinged with Winter's frosts; the tree
stands about 35 cm (14 in) high
(photograph by R H Cuthbert)

a

b

43

45 'Willowhay' by Margaret
Suckling, a highly textured panel in
many tones of yellow and green with
machine stitchery, hanging wools and
three-dimensional leaves depicting the
rich colours of Autumn (photograph
by R H Cuthbert)

46 'Summer Garden' by Beryl
Morgan shows a bird's eye view of a
lawn surrounded by brilliant flowers
of red, yellow, blues, pinks and white
with green foliage; the lawn is of
green towelling fabric around which
are small areas of applied nets and
embroidered eyelets (photograph by
V A Harding)

47 *Right* The cold weather dries the hedgerows and grasses leaving only the tenacious ivy clinging to the centre surrounded by a tangled mass of prickly branches – note the rich pattern of delicately crossed lines covering heavier textures underneath (photograph by Jean Littlejohn)

48 *Below* The Autumn sun filters through the branches, dappling the trunks and ground with patches of light (photograph by R H Cuthbert)

49 (a) *Right, Above* 'Winter Tree' by Elizabeth Davies, one of two panels depicting the same tree in Winter and in Summer; this one, worked on a white background overlaid with soft grey and brown nets shows the stark contrast of tones (photograph by V A Harding)

(b) *Right, below* 'Summer Tree' by Elizabeth Davies is the second of two panels showing the same tree at different seasons; this one is flooded with bright sunlight making a vivid splash of colour against a dull background * the rich textures in the foreground suggest a lush growth of green and yellow (photograph by V A Harding)

50 Trees in Winter show the delicate lace patterns made by bare branches against the sky, but reflecting a softened image in the glassy water (photograph by R H Cuthbert)

51 The first frosts leave their mark on foliage still moist from Summer and, by freezing the water inside the veins, shrivel the leaves and lightly powder them with crispy white (photograph by V A Harding)

1 'Patchwork Morning' by Jan Messent. A three-dimensional patchwork cat sits on the windowsill looking out into a sunlit patchwork garden. Some patches are padded and stitched on top of others. (Photograph by Gail Bathgate)

2 'M'Lady"s Packhorse' by Jan Messent. Machine appliqué with three-dimensional packs and other details, made for exhibition in schools to illustrate how children could participate in a group project requiring many small parts. (Photograph by Gail Bathgate)

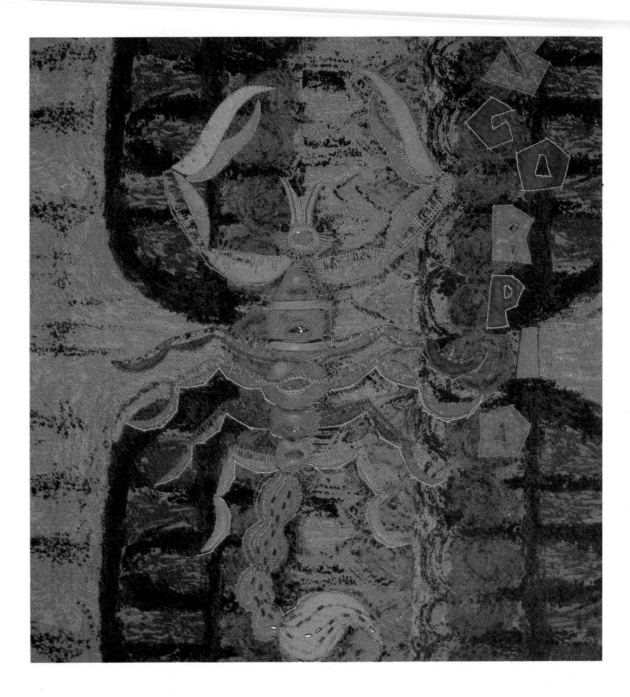

3 'Scorpio' by Jane Lemon, using
appliqué, padded leather shapes and
stitchery. Embroidered on a patterned
fabric, a creature may be perfectly
camouflaged as it would be in its natural
surroundings. (Photograph by Gail
Bathgate)

52 'Winter Frost' by Jean Parry
depicting the effect of heavy frost on
lacy larch trees. Glass beads have
been attached to catch the light as it
is seen from different angles
(photograph by V A Harding)

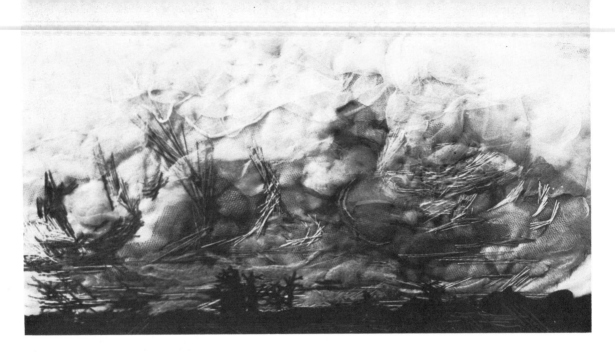

53 *Above* 'Winter Sunset' by Christine Andrews shows swirling, heavy clouds tinged with crimson and pink; use has been made of chiffon and nets, overlaid, padded and accented with straight stitches – the dark silhouette of the landscape lends a sense of foreboding to the scene (photograph by V A Harding)

54 'Cairngorms in Winter' by Julie Athill: a small panel worked almost entirely in white, relying on different textures for interest (photograph by V A Harding)

55 *Right* This frozen waterfall would be an exciting starting point for an embroidery in sparkling white, grey, blue and darker contrasts; rich textures could be created by needleweaving, cutwork and pulled work (photograph by Sarah Harding)

Nature in Monochrome

Monochrome means 'of one colour'. The pure colour is called a hue; various tones of one colour are achieved by adding white to obtain a tint or by adding black to obtain a shade. There can be many tones of one colour ranging from the very palest to the very darkest, as there are tones of grey ranging from white to black. A 'colour scheme' based on tones of one colour is therefore called a monochrome scheme, but this should not be confused with monotone which means 'only one tone'. An embroidery worked in monotone could be quilted, where the surface of the fabric is held down to create shadows and highlights, or in surface stitchery using all white threads. There are many variations on this theme.

To limit oneself to the use of only one colour in embroidery can be demanding and rewarding, relying as it does on carefully placed areas of textures, shapes and patterns. Although techniques such as blackwork, pulled thread and cutwork were traditionally executed in monochrome, the rules are now often relaxed to allow for more individual experimentation.

Nature provides many good examples of monochromatic schemes; for example, a foggy day when everything around us loses its colour and becomes tones of grey. A leafy glade suffused with green light filtering between mossy boulders and fern fronds is reflected in the green water of a still pond. Snow scenes, animal camouflage, silhouettes and minerals also provide ideas.

The following is a list of embroidery techniques which look especially well in monochrome:

Pulled work, Cut work, Hardanger, Drawn thread	The surface of the fabric is changed by pulling or cutting holes, with the addition of stitch patterns.
Quilting, Padding, Smocking	The fabric is manipulated into areas of high relief.
Metal thread work	Relies for effect on the play of light and shade on the direction of the threads.
Blackwork	Patterns of stitches of varying density.
Assisi work	Cross stitches worked in negative areas, design left void.
Surface stitchery, Appliqué, Canvas work	Areas of contrasting texture created by stitches or fabric.

56 Cloud banks seen from above provide the starting point for a design in blackwork, or for quilting, appliqué and padding in tones of one colour (photograph by R H Cuthbert)

57 Textures of one colour show how the areas of highest relief in the foreground suggest a nearness which contrasts with the lower padding and quilting in the distance (photograph by R H Cuthbert)

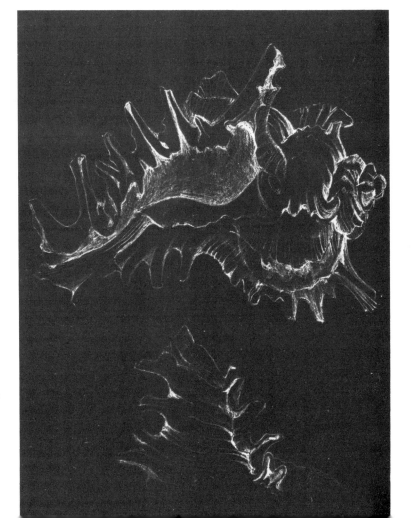

58 The negative print of a drawing may produce quite a different effect from that of the original, lighting those places which were in shadow – this drawing suggests white machine embroidery on a dark fabric (photograph by Gail Bathgate)

54

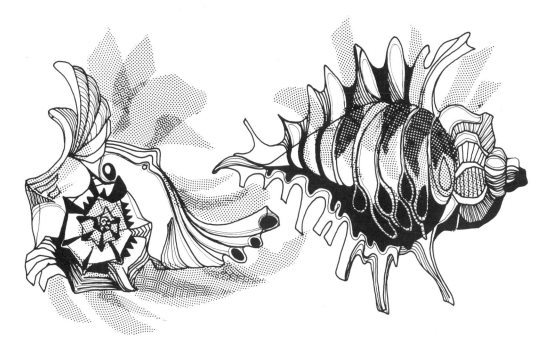

59 (a) A pen drawing of a shell may be given extra tones by the addition of transfer (e.g. Letraset) patterns; this is a useful way of designing for blackwork as the various patterns on the papers may suggest stitches like those used in this technique

(b) Blackwork stitches show the range of tones made by using a heavier thread and denser stitches, gradually lightening to finer thread and thinly scattered stitches (photograph by David Prout)

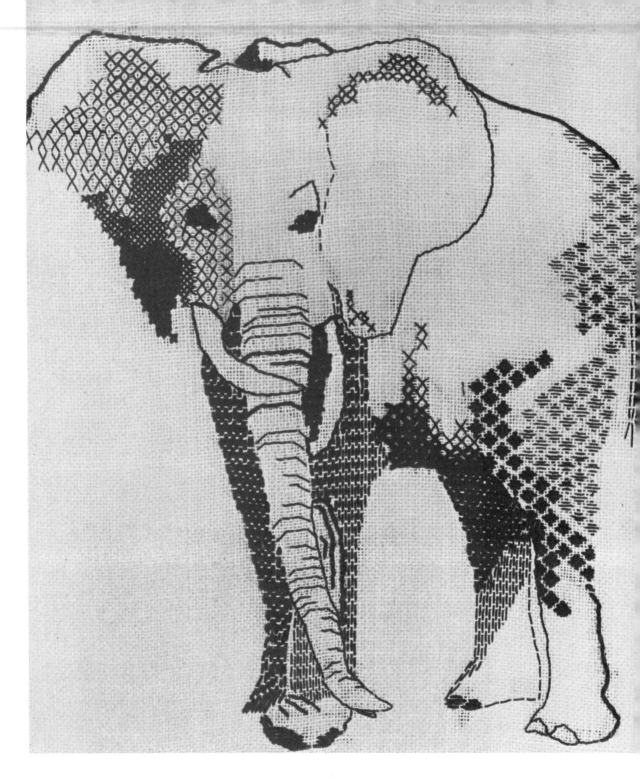

60 'Blackwork Elephant' by Jill
Friend shows how tonal effects are
achieved by the use of thick and thin
threads and by denser stitch patterns
in the darker areas (photograph by
R H Cuthbert)

56

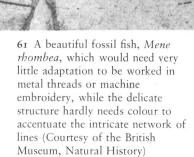

61 A beautiful fossil fish, *Mene rhombea*, which would need very little adaptation to be worked in metal threads or machine embroidery, while the delicate structure hardly needs colour to accentuate the intricate network of lines (Courtesy of the British Museum, Natural History)

62 Machine embroidery experiment by Valerie Harding to capture the pattern seen on a flat fish – a small amount of hand embroidery is also included; this motif, arranged five or six times within a circle with the tails at the centre, would make a design for a cushion (photograph by V A Harding)

57

63 *Right* The arrangement of plates on a seahorse would make this design perfect for padded appliqué in one colour, or quilting: it could be used as a single motif on a garment, or placed at one side of a table mat worked in one colour on a matching fabric

64 *Below* Studied closely, insects prove to be very beautiful, and if we can overcome our prejudice against them having 'too many legs' we can find much about them to recommend their use in design; they adapt to all types of monochrome embroidery as shown by this example of pulled work by Freda Stoneman, worked on coarse linen scrim (photograph by Norman Weston)

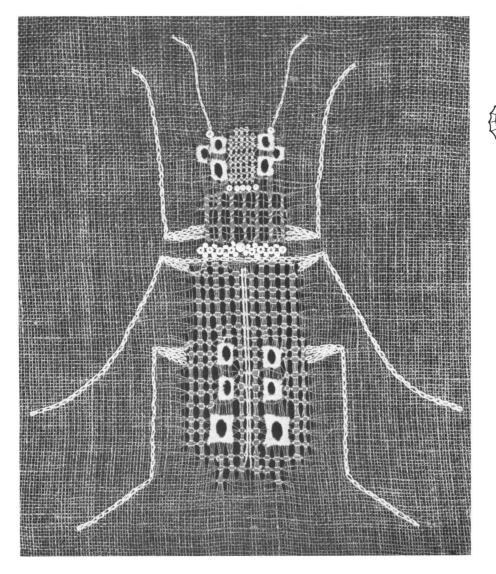

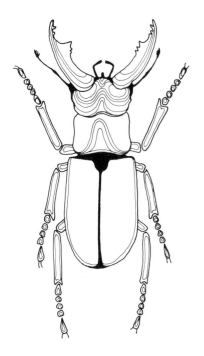

65 *Above right* Shadow work insect by Beryl Court, worked on fine white lawn in white thread (photograph by Norman Weston)

66 *Above left* This handsome stag beetle, with its body of shining armour, could be worked in padded leather appliqué, perhaps in silver kid with silver thread for the smaller details

67 Transparency in the wings of a dragonfly can be achieved by using layers of organza, nylon net and delicate transparent fabrics with metal threads, tiny beads and sequins – the accent should be on delicacy and fragility

68 'Cutwork Butterfly' by Sheila Kinross; this method gives an impression of airiness to the design and would be a suitable decoration for a tray cloth or tablecloth, or as the decoration on the yoke of a dress (photograph by Norman Weston)

69 Machine cutwork fish by Jackey Hill, showing another way of achieving delicacy in one colour (photograph by Norman Weston)

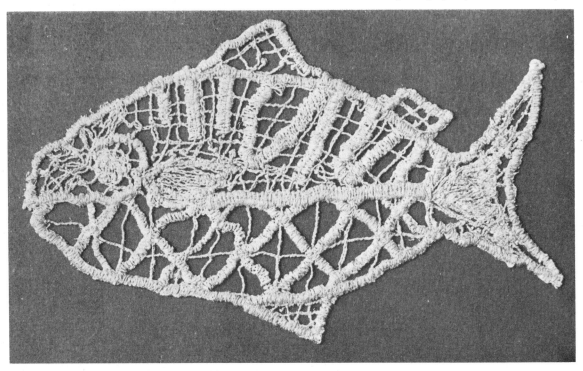

70 Owl, in Hardanger embroidery by Sheila Kinross; this method is a combination of cutwork and needleweaving worked in squares – it is traditionally worked in one colour, relying for effect on the areas of holes and textures (photograph by Norman Weston)

71 Pattern of cross stitch dragons, by Jackey Hill – worked on a coarse evenweave linen in one colour, these motifs would make a charming decoration in a child's bedroom (photograph by Norman Weston)

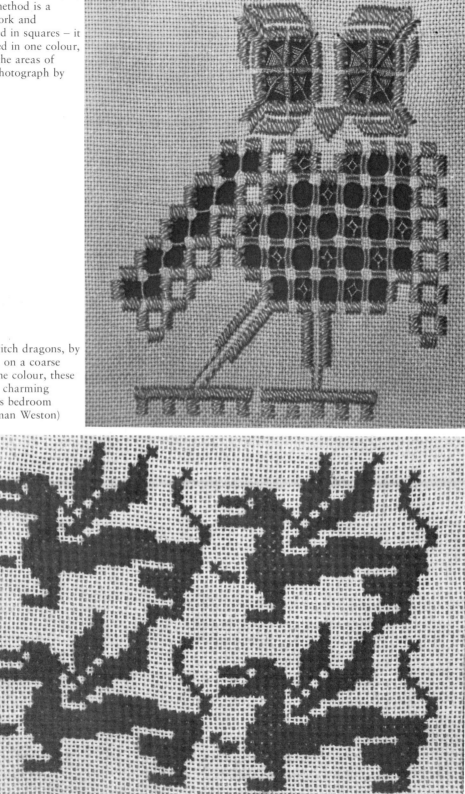

72 *Left* A misty November morning, the sun barely showing up the outline of trees and hedge (photograph by R H Cuthbert)

73 (**a** and **b**) *Below and Above right* A set of four table mats with matching glass mats designed by the author and embroidered by Linda Nichol, worked in coffee-coloured stranded cotton on coarse evenweave linen in cross stitch, the glass mats have the colours reversed and show the matching leaves for each tree (photograph by R H Cuthbert)

74 *Below right and overleaf* The mats were worked on coarse linen, 7 threads to the centimetre (18 threads to the inch), the large mats measuring 30 × 21.5 cm (12 × 8½ in) and the glass mats measuring 11.5 × 11.5 cm (4½ × 4½ in); each stitch was worked over two threads in each direction
(**a**) Field Maple
(**b**) Horse Chestnut
(**c**) Apple
(**d**) Holly

a

b

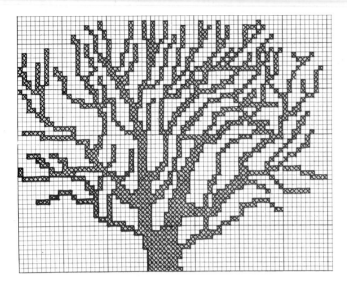

c

d

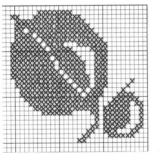

74 (contd). See page 62

75 *Left* Hosta leaves (photograph by V A Harding)

76 A green silk quilted cushion by Millicent Spiller: the design was based on leaf shapes and the regular pattern of veins like those seen on the hosta (photograph by R H Cuthbert)

77 *Right* A pencil sketch of geranium leaves shown as negative shapes, the interest being centred on the stalks; when drawing a plant in this way, it is easier to eliminate the details by having the light behind it

78 Some creatures have distinctive shapes which can be successfully left unworked while the background receives the decorative treatment – this is called voiding

79 'Dragon' shadow quilting by Jackey Hill: deeper tones of felt are cut out and laid between two layers of fine semi-transparent fabric; fine backstitching round the shapes keeps the sandwiched felt in place, at the same time producing a quilted effect (photograph by Norman Weston)

80 'The Blue Boar' by Valerie Harding, a design based on a local inn sign and used on the embroidered cover of a book compiled by local members of the Women's Institute. The blue boar is worked in padded kid, suede and fabric and applied to a background of blue hessian (burlap) – the lines created by the sections indicate the natural flow of lines on the body; this is a satisfactory method of designing with animals, and is open to a wide variety of embroidery techniques (photograph by V A Harding)

Pattern in Nature

81 *Facing page* (a) *Top left* A pattern of Rose of Sharon leaves, strong, waxy and pointing in all directions – the leaves could be embroidered using satin stitch, Roumanian couching or cretan stitch (photograph by Judith Milne)
(b) *Top right* Straight, spear-like leaves make an interesting pattern with spaces between; lay a piece of tracing paper over the photograph and plot out these spaces before embroidering them on fabric in straight stitches (photograph by Judith Milne)
(c) *Bottom right* A pattern of 'quilted' leaves with tiny bunches of bead-like flowers showing here and there (photograph by Judith Milne)
(d) *Bottom left* Variegated ivy makes a pattern with a strong downwards direction: look at the illustration with half-closed eyes to find a possible blackwork design – the pattern on the leaves would give ample scope for stitch variations (see figure 240) (photograph by V A Harding)

Pattern results from the repetition of units and motifs whether of different sizes, repeated haphazardly, in a formal structure or as *part of* the structure – as in the pattern of a bird's feathers. Nature abounds with pattern, from the lowest forms of life to the most sophisticated. Plants with thick foliage make an informal pattern of repeated shapes, a lawn covered with daisies, the fur and skin patterns of animals, honeycomb, a cluster of barnacles or tomatoes, frogspawn: the examples are endless.

Apart from those patterns which occur naturally, there are also potential design motifs in nature which lend themselves perfectly to repetition either because of their symmetry, their simplicity or their beautiful shapes. The insect world is full of such motifs; useful too are footprints, fish, birds and flowers. Indeed, these have been printed and woven on textiles as patterns for centuries and are still popular today.

Ideas for pattern in embroidery can be tried in all techniques and styles, even those which appear to rely on colour-changes (as in a tiger's skin) could be worked in one colour only, using a change of *texture* to indicate the pattern. A crocodile's skin, which is a pattern of raised areas in one colour, could be worked in raised stitches in complementary colours, or in cutwork to show a patterned fabric underneath.

Study nature's patterns closely and from them glean ideas of the various structures in which the units are repeated, some of which are shown here. These may provide a basis for patchwork projects or for appliqué and stitch patterns. Canvaswork, particularly, is made up of stitch patterns, as also are blackwork and pulled work. These may be useful starting points for those who would like to explore this aspect of nature in more detail.

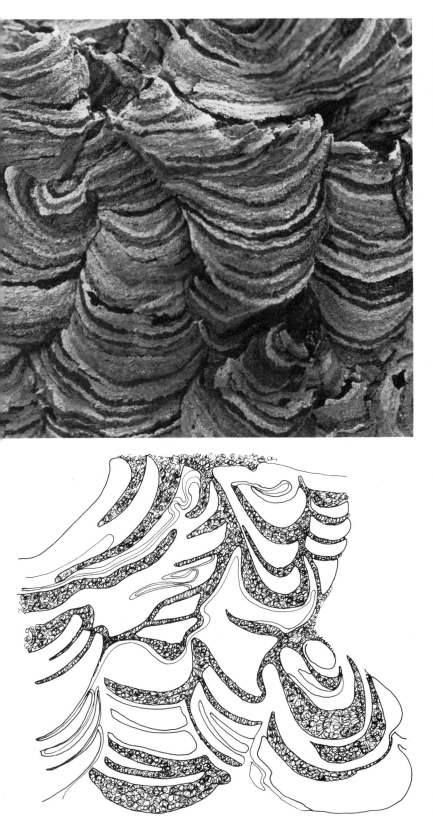

82 (a) A wasps' nest makes a complex pattern of swirling lines within curved shapes from which numerous designs could be formed. Each larger shape could be taken separately and used as a pattern for padded quilting, or lines could be followed for a goldwork or couched design (photograph by V A Harding)

(b) A simple design using some of the swirling shapes and lines seen on the wasps' nest

83 Patchwork-type patterns are often seen on fish and mammals, reptiles and amphibians: those seen here are from the plates on a snake's head, the teeth of a shark-nosed ray, markings on the plates of a sea-lily, the plates on a tortoise's carapace and a section of a fossil sea-urchin; they suggest ideas for patchwork construction, both formal and informal, and for lines of quilting on top

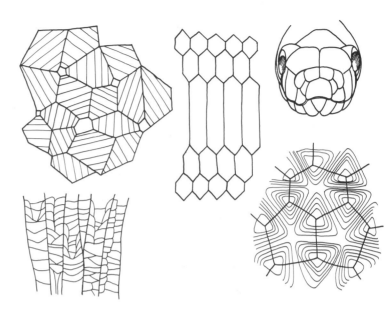

84 A similar hexagonal construction of patches is used here as a decoration on children's clothes, designed and worked by Heide Jenkins (photograph by V A Harding)

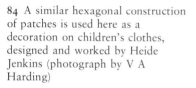

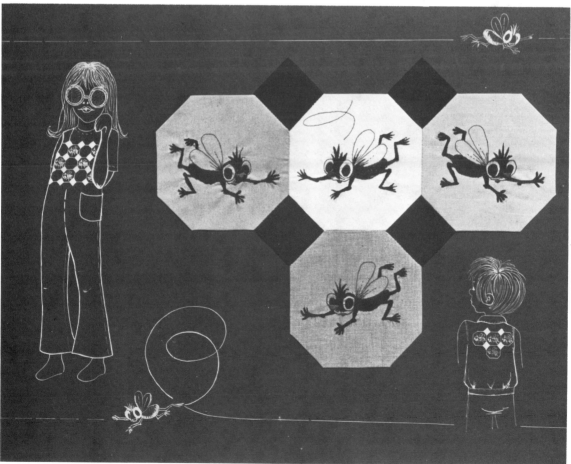

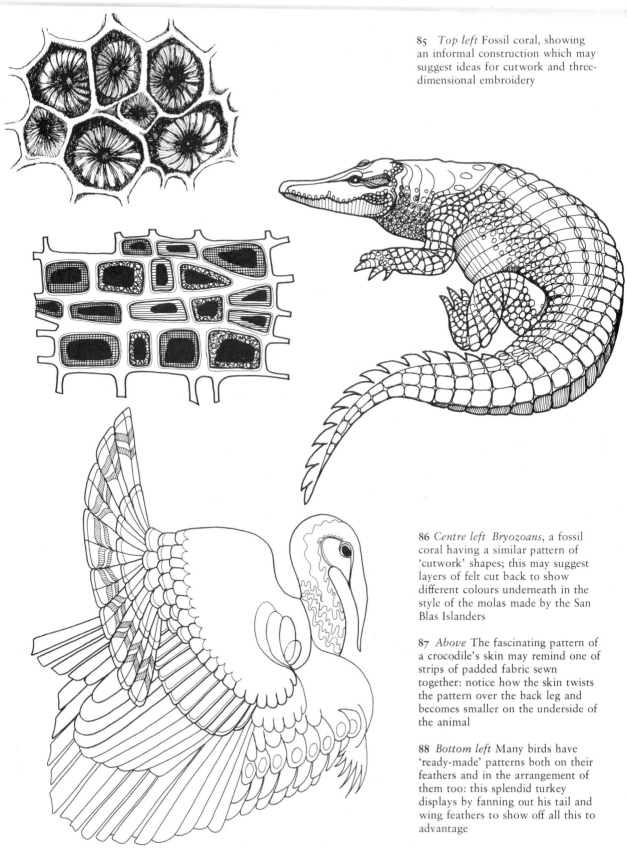

85 *Top left* Fossil coral, showing an informal construction which may suggest ideas for cutwork and three-dimensional embroidery

86 *Centre left* Bryozoans, a fossil coral having a similar pattern of 'cutwork' shapes; this may suggest layers of felt cut back to show different colours underneath in the style of the molas made by the San Blas Islanders

87 *Above* The fascinating pattern of a crocodile's skin may remind one of strips of padded fabric sewn together: notice how the skin twists the pattern over the back leg and becomes smaller on the underside of the animal

88 *Bottom left* Many birds have 'ready-made' patterns both on their feathers and in the arrangement of them too: this splendid turkey displays by fanning out his tail and wing feathers to show off all this to advantage

4 'Flower Heads' by Barbara Buttle.
Canvaswork; one of the flowers is three-
dimensional. (Photograph by V A
Harding)

5 'Mola Waistcoat' by Audrey Ormrod, made in the technique used by the Cuna Indians of the San Blas Islands, Panama, and designed by the embroiderer in the style and brilliant colours traditional to these people. (Photograph by Gail Bathgate).

89 The stitches of canvas embroidery make patterns which can be used to good effect when chosen with care; look carefully at your design source to find the natural areas of pattern, and translate these into stitches taking into consideration the direction of the pattern, the scale and the texture

90 Canvaswork stitches were used to introduce pattern on this ostrich by Jan Messent – the mixture of free and formal stitchery blends together well; grey, black, white and silver wool and cotton threads are used on Winchester canvas (photograph by Norman Weston)

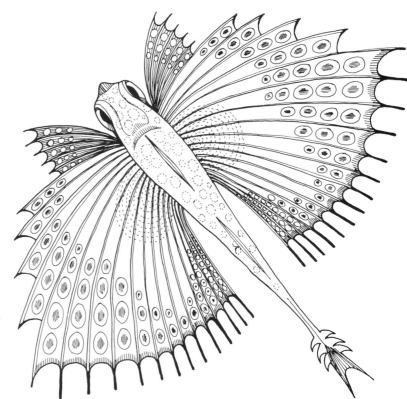

91 Flying fish with open pectoral fins showing an impressive pattern of shapes

92 Canvaswork orange and gold fish by Jan Messent (photograph by V A Harding)

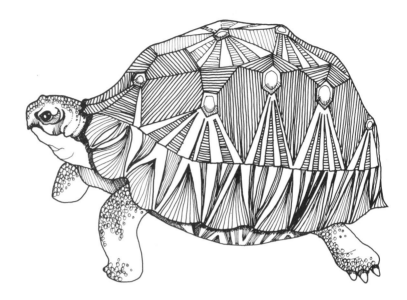

93 Radiated tortoise, with outstanding pattern markings on the carapace

94 'Goldwork Tortoise' by Valerie Harding: the segments on the carapace are highly padded gold kid, and the rough texture on the head and legs is couched in gold thread and purl (photograph by V A Harding)

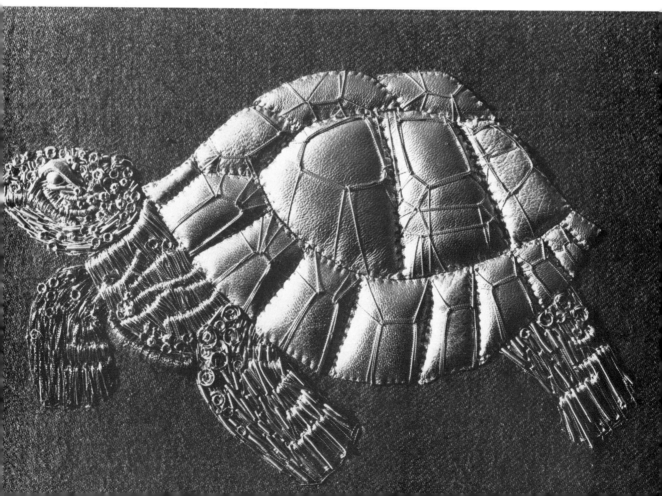

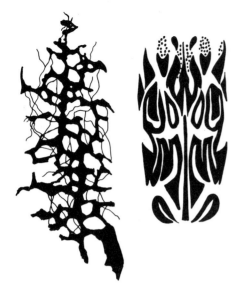

95 *Above* Patterns from beetles' wing cases could be used for experiments of a formal or informal nature in various embroidery techniques

96 *Above right* Fly stitch in various sizes and threads used with beads to suggest the pattern seen on a seashell (photograph by Gail Bathgate)

97 *Below left* The pattern of an ocelot, one of the smaller and most beautifully marked members of the cat family, would need some adaptation before being used as an embroidery design

98 *Below right* A formal interpretation of the pattern on a cat's fur, similar to the natural one which follows the curve of the back: this is a good position from which to see the pattern on both the back and the face at the same time

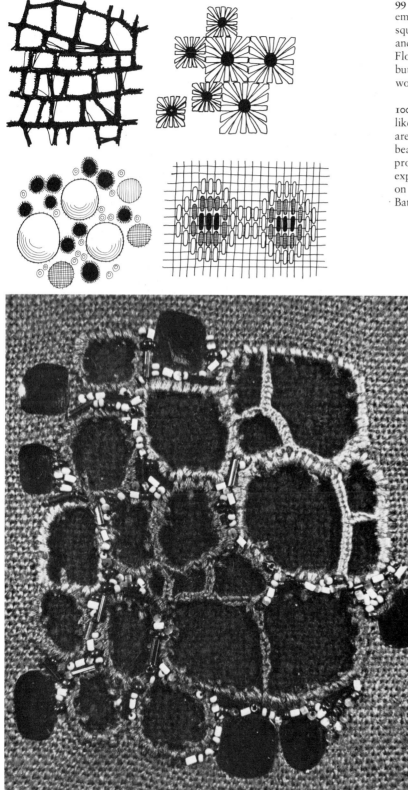

99 Spot patterns can be created in embroidery by using needleweaving, square eyelets, padded circles, cut and bound holes with beads and Florentine stitch on canvas; buttonhole wheels and spider's webs would also create a similar effect

100 Experiment to produce a spot-like pattern in cutwork – the holes are bound roughly with cotton, while beads and shiny plastic leather pieces provide highlights; try a small experiment to reproduce the pattern on a cat's fur (photograph by Gail Bathgate)

101 Pattern on the skin of a tabby cat

102 All zebra's stripes are different, even those within the same species: see how they vary and how they move as the animal moves. The mane stands upright from the neck and the stripes continue through it; the tail is quite different from that of the horse, and the stripes continue down that also

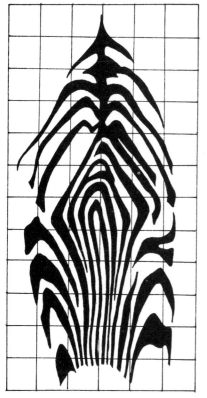

103 The markings on a zebra's face

104 The same design is enlarged by dividing a rectangle of the required size into the number of squares, and copying the lines seen within each small square into the larger ones. On this enlargement, the design has been marked in black, white and grey to add interest. From this arrangement a block of squares may be selected and used as the basis of a design. In this way, use could be made of patterned and plain fabric together, with quilting, couching and stitchery, padding and appliqué

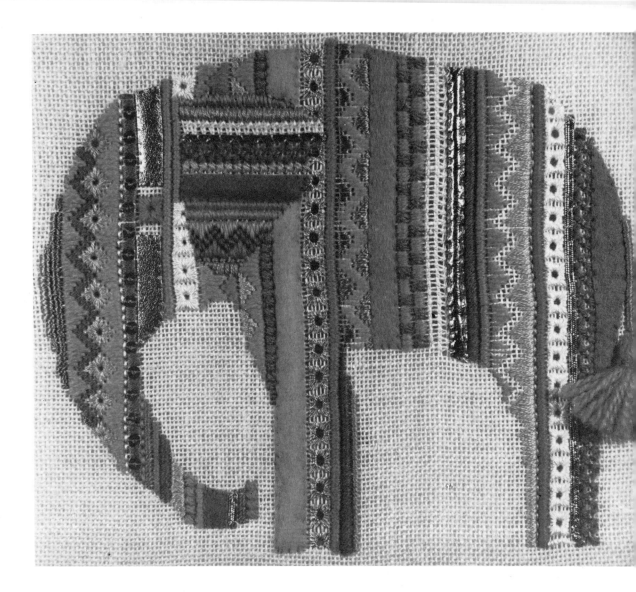

105 A 'fun' design of an elephant by Jan Messent, worked in stripes of various kinds, using canvaswork stitches, pulled work, appliqué and cross stitch. On coarse linen, all the threads are orange, yellow and gold; the ear is marked by stripes worked horizontally (photograph by Gail Bathgate)

106 A pattern of penguins, showing only the black parts – they are still recognisable like this and would make a charming border pattern

107 A graceful antelope seen as a series of shapes which lead the viewer's eye from the tip of the horns, down the neck, along the body and down the legs; the small area of pattern on the underbody links with that on the face as a contrast to the otherwise plain design

108 An experiment using different sized checks to suggest distance, the theory being that objects nearest the observer will appear larger than those further away: this idea would make an interesting border on a child's bedspread or curtains (photograph by David Prout)

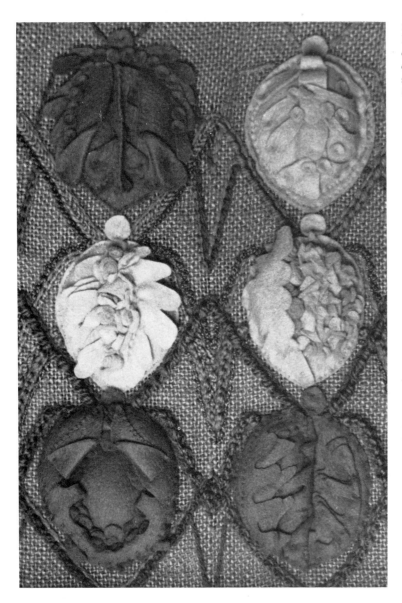

109 An experimental pattern by Jean Beebe of beetles in orange felts and couched threads, each of which has a different texture made by cutting and sewing the felt in various ways (photograph by Norman Weston)

110 *Above right* Pattern of tiny feather shapes by Heide Jenkins: each one is treated differently and would make an interesting decoration on an evening dress worked in shiny threads, beads and sequins

111 *Below right* A similar formation of shapes based on eggshells, in quilting, by Jill Friend (photograph by Norman Weston)

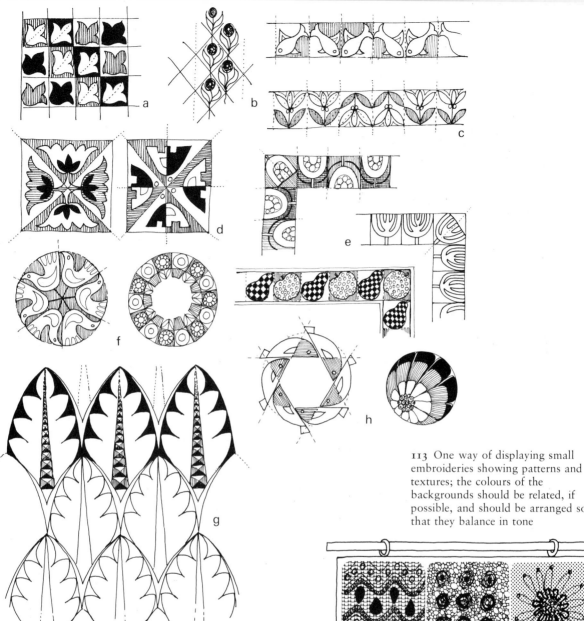

112 Some ways of repeating a motif for a border, allover pattern, square or circle
(a) Square grid pattern
(b) Diagonal grid pattern
(c) Squared borders
(d) Squares of four and eight sections
(e) Some ways of turning a corner
(f) A motif repeated inside a circle
(g) Leaf shapes carved in a stone column
(h) Arrangements in circles

113 One way of displaying small embroideries showing patterns and textures; the colours of the backgrounds should be related, if possible, and should be arranged so that they balance in tone

84

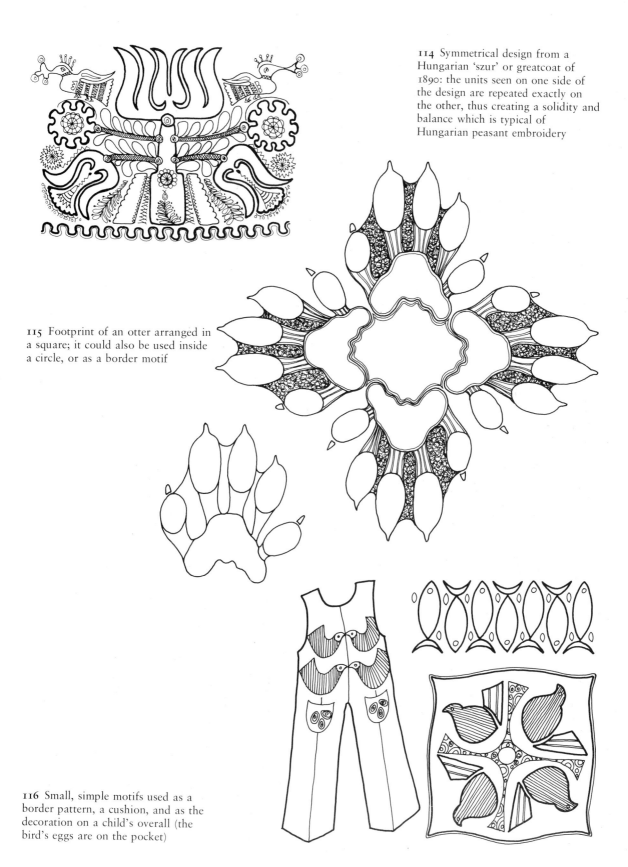

114 Symmetrical design from a Hungarian 'szur' or greatcoat of 1890: the units seen on one side of the design are repeated exactly on the other, thus creating a solidity and balance which is typical of Hungarian peasant embroidery

115 Footprint of an otter arranged in a square; it could also be used inside a circle, or as a border motif

116 Small, simple motifs used as a border pattern, a cushion, and as the decoration on a child's overall (the bird's eggs are on the pocket)

Nature's Circles

As designers of embroidery, we are fortunate in having nature provide us with an abundance of motifs which fit so easily into one of our favourite shapes, the circle. How many times have we looked for suitable ideas for a box top, a stool, a circular tray-cloth or mat, a cushion or an embroidered rug?

Nature's circles appear to fall into three main categories: the segmented, or radiating circle, the spiral and the circle composed of concentric rings. Other almost symmetrical designs within a circle can be found in cross sections of some fruits, but in the other three types, the formation of the circle shows the direction of the growth.

1   *Radiating circles*
    some microscopic organisms
    snowflakes
    flower heads
    cross sections of some fruit and minerals
    some shells and limpets
    some fossils
    mushroom gills

2   *Spirals*
    snails and some shells
    some fossils, particularly ammonites
    animal horns
    fern fronds
    pine cones
    the galaxies
    some micro-organisms

3   *Concentric circles*   bracket fungi
    dried seed heads   some corals and minerals, e.g.
    cross sections of trees   malachite and jasper
    cross sections of onions   eye spots on feathers and insect
    some lichens   wings
    ripples on water
    planet rings

117 *Below* Limpets with radiating ridges; the lower one has barnacles growing on it

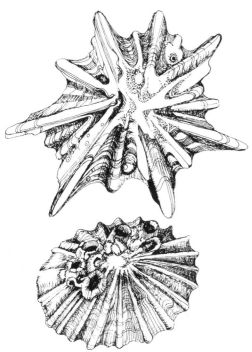

118 *Right* Snowflakes make delightful motifs for embroidery, as all are based on a six-pointed figure and no two are exactly alike

119 A section of a compact coral colony known as *Lithostrotion arachnoidium*; the radiating lines form a patchwork-like pattern

120 *Left* Fossil sea-urchins have knob-like radiating arms

121 Needleweaving experiment based on a microscopic organism (photograph by V A Harding)

122 *Left* Minute micro-organisms used as an experiment for circles in padded leather, rings, metal threads, beads and sequins (photograph by David Prout)

123 Frost touches the radiating stalks of a garden plant and encrusts it thickly with glittering crystals (photograph by V A Harding)

124 Succulent (photograph by V A Harding)

125 Many fruit and vegetable cross sections are circular and highly decorative; they make good motifs for repeating patterns, and with careful study provide ample material for more detailed embroideries

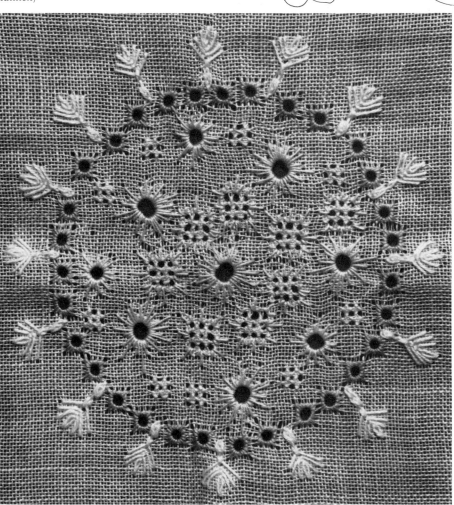

126 'Dandelion Clock', a pulled thread design worked by Barbara Snook on Norland linen in coton á broder (photograph by John Hunnex)

127 Microscopic organisms, many of which are circular, suggest techniques such as needleweaving, goldwork, cutwork and stitchery with beads and sequins

128 A border design in the Art Nouveau style by S Winifred Rhodes, 1894: spiral snail shells and foliage in sinuous forms (courtesy of Dover Publications)

130 Concentric rings can clearly be seen in this cross section of a mineral; there are many ways of using a design like this, with couched threads, string and cords, layers of felt cut back to show the layer underneath, or layers of fabric or kid piled up and padded

129 An ammonite (a spiral fossil) simplified for an embroidery design using padded appliqué, cutwork and jewels to give an impression of three levels

131 (a) A dried seedhead, frayed and split round the edges with both radiating and concentric lines (photograph by Norman Weston)

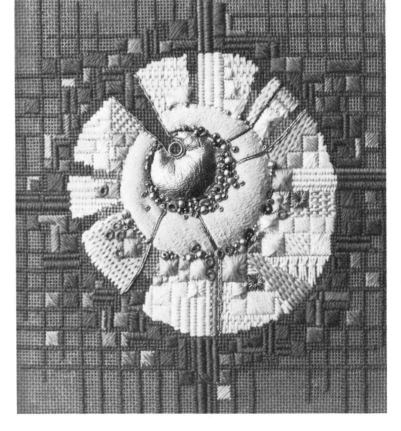

(b) 'Seed Head' canvas embroidery by Jan Messent, based on the seedhead shown in (a). The natural colours of cream, white and yellow were used, with padded chamois leather and gold kid, metal threads and beads. The canvas was painted and left partly unworked to lessen the textural effect towards the edges (photograph by Norman Weston)

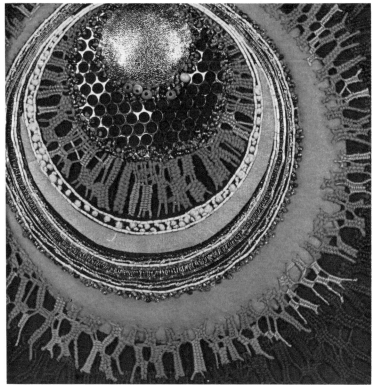

132 A design of concentric circles by Judith Milne, based on the sun: gold kid, yellow and beige felt on brown, needleweaving, couching and beads (photograph by Norman Weston)

133 Circles of lichen (photograph by Jennifer Gray)

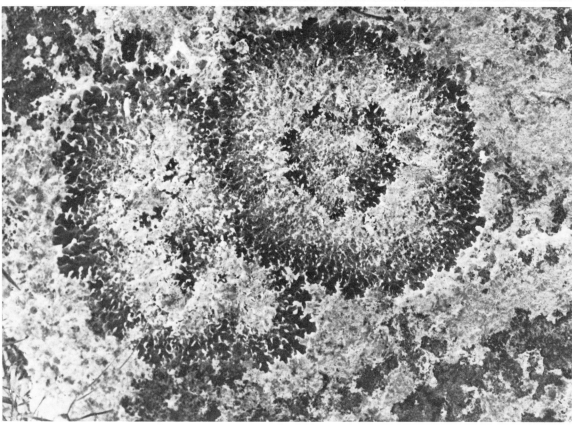

Texture in Nature

Texture and pattern are often confused, which is hardly surprising since they are often inseparable, especially in nature. The quality which makes texture different is that it can be described by the *tactile* nature of its surfaces, that is, its degree of roughness or smoothness or any other way in which the surface deviates from the flat, rather than by a visual arrangement of units alone. A texture can be *felt*, whereas a pattern alone (though sometimes textural too) must be *seen* to be appreciated. Thus the chapters on pattern and texture will inevitably overlap as nature so often arranges that texture on some things (such as crocodile skins, pine cones and pineapples) also forms a pattern.

It should be understood, of course, that *everything* has a texture whether it is smooth, silky, velvety, satiny, shiny, bumpy or rough. Such areas of smoothness and calm are needed as a foil to the more highly textured areas which tend to attract most attention. Without these contrasting textures a piece of work may easily become too 'busy'.

Experiment with these ways of creating texture:

1 Distort fabric by smocking, 'scrunching', padding and quilting, pleating, making coils, twists and rolls of fabric, applying pieces of fabric-covered card.

2 Change the nature of the fabric by cutting holes, fraying, drawing and pulling threads.

3 Use fabrics with exciting textures such as shiny, plastic-coated fabric, leather, fur fabric, velvet, satin, scrim, hessian (burlap), silk, tweed, chiffon, net, lurex and corduroy.

4 Attach three-dimensional objects to the fabric: beads, wood and metal pieces, buttons, washers, rings, studs, jewels, stones, shi-sha glass, plastic and wooden tubing, dowel, wire, feathers and shells.

5 Use different threads: textured bumpy wool, handspun yarn, string, cord, fine crochet thread, machine and button thread, rug wool, thread unravelled from fabric.

6 Experiment with stitches: French and bullion knots, Astrakhan

(velvet) stitch, satin stitch, Rhodes stitch (for canvaswork), raised chain band, seeding, straight stitch, cretan stitch.

7   Use other textile techniques with embroidery to create different effects: knitting, crochet, hairpin crochet, tatting, macramé and off-loom weaving.

134 Shell mosaic of the brachiopod *Terebratella dorsata* from the south Atlantic, magnified six hundred times; strips of felt, finely pleated fabric of thick lines of raised stitchery could be used to reconstruct this pattern or ridges and holes (courtesy of the British Museum, Natural History)

135 The magnified structure of an animal bone suggests needleweaving or two layers of cutwork

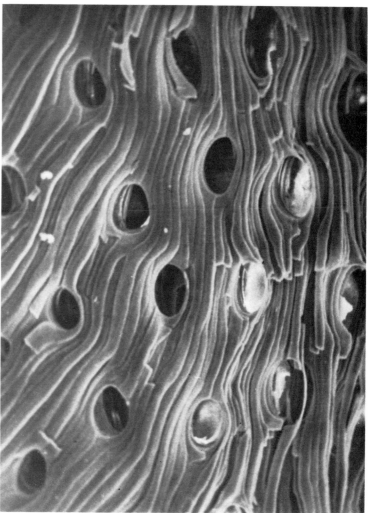

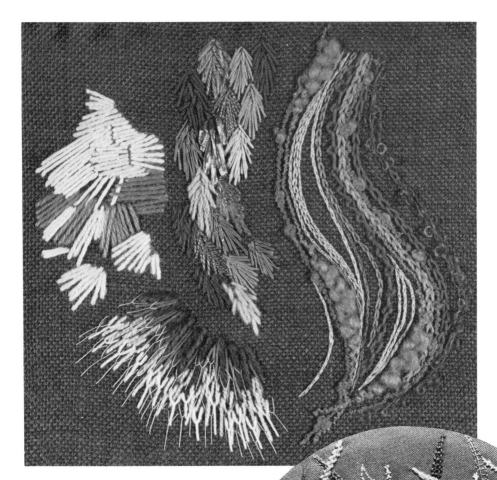

136 A stitchery experiment to simulate the textures of fur and hair, using straight stitches, couching, fly stitch and chain stitch (photograph by Gail Bathgate)

137 'Beetle' by Heide Jenkins, worked in padded leather and suede on leaves of raised stitches making a marked contrast in texture (photograph by V A Harding)

138 Cast-off snake's skin
(photograph by V A Harding)

139 The ribbed, dorsal side of a sea-urchin has a texture of small and large bumps set into separate compartments; this may suggest a construction of card-covered pieces fitted together and scattered with beads, sequins and French knots

140 *Right* Some patterns and textures seen on shells, suggesting a variety of experiments with torn leather, frayed fabric and machine embroidery

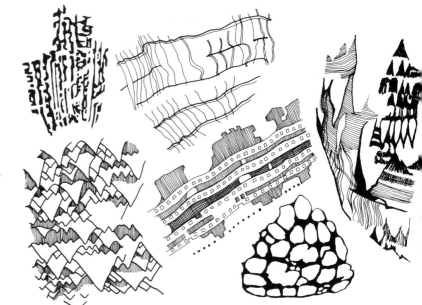

141 (**a** and **b**) *Below left* This texture from the cap of a fungus is remarkably similar to that of the brain coral – both resemble ruched velvet or gathers of crochet sewn together

142 *Below right* Detail of sea-anemone tentacles

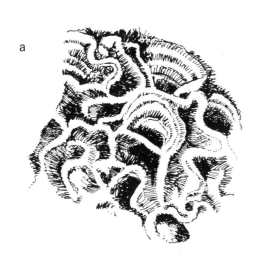

a

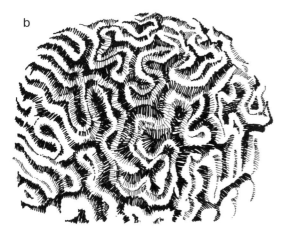

b

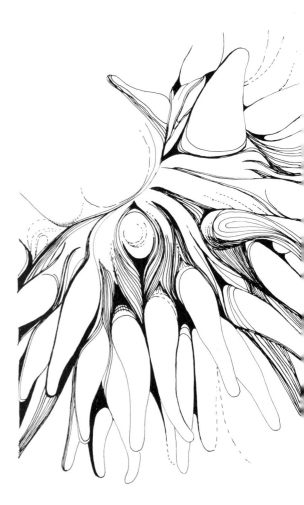

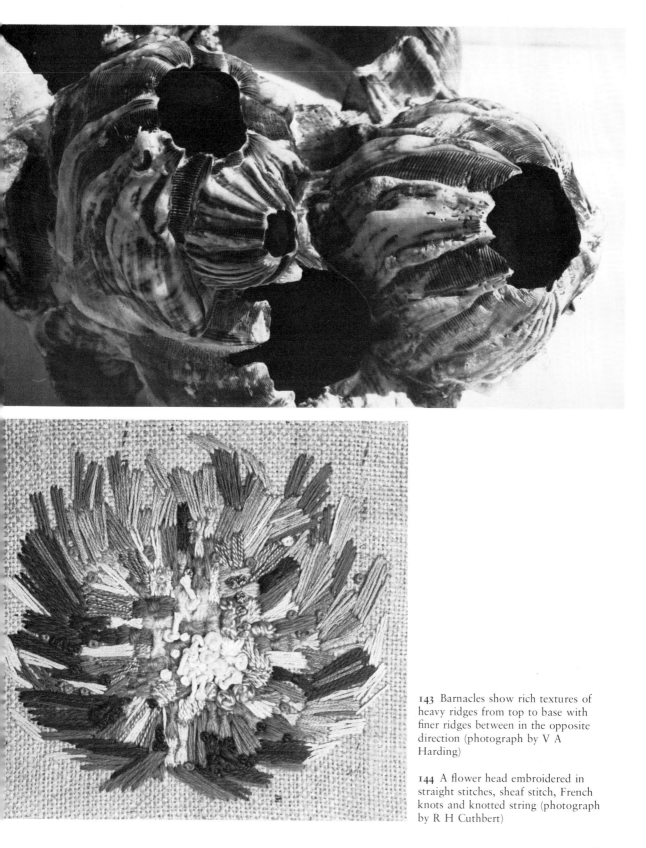

143 Barnacles show rich textures of heavy ridges from top to base with finer ridges between in the opposite direction (photograph by V A Harding)

144 A flower head embroidered in straight stitches, sheaf stitch, French knots and knotted string (photograph by R H Cuthbert)

145 *Above* The bole of a palm tree, with ragged, papery strips peeling away (photograph by Barbara Snook)

146 *Above right* Paper-bark Maple also has peeling strips hanging from it: this can clearly be seen as fabric, showing both sides, slashed and rolled to give the same effect (photograph by V A Harding)

147 *Facing page* Three-dimensional panel by Diana Seidl, based on thickly growing foliage; highly padded layers of towelling give an impression of depth, upon which are built padded and cut-out felt leaf shapes (photograph by R H Cuthbert)

148 The corduroy-like appearance of
a cork oak bark (photograph by V A
Harding)

149 Ridges made by heavy chain
stitch between patches of suede,
straight stitches and metal threads
(photograph by Gail Bathgate)

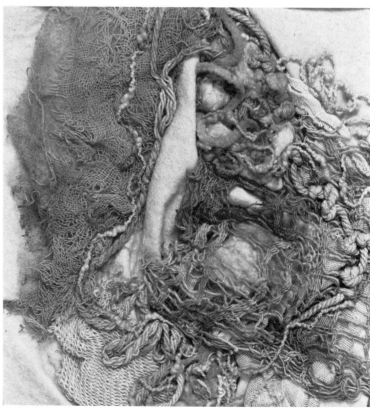

150 The gnarled, twisting roots of trees make an exciting texture in three dimensions (photograph by V A Harding)

151 An experiment in textures by Diana Seidl, which recreates the gnarled tree roots seen in figure 150 (photograph by R H Cuthbert)

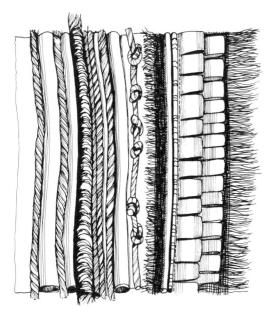

152 *Above* The textural nature of a fabric can be altered in many ways; this shows some of the methods by which ridges can be made: couched string, knotted and straight, corded quilting, pleating and snipped pleats

153 *Right* Trees in winter (photograph by Jean Littlejohn)

154 *Far right* 'The Tree' by Freda Stoneman, pulled work on coarse white linen of a design inspired by the bare branches of a tree in winter (photograph by R H Cuthbert)

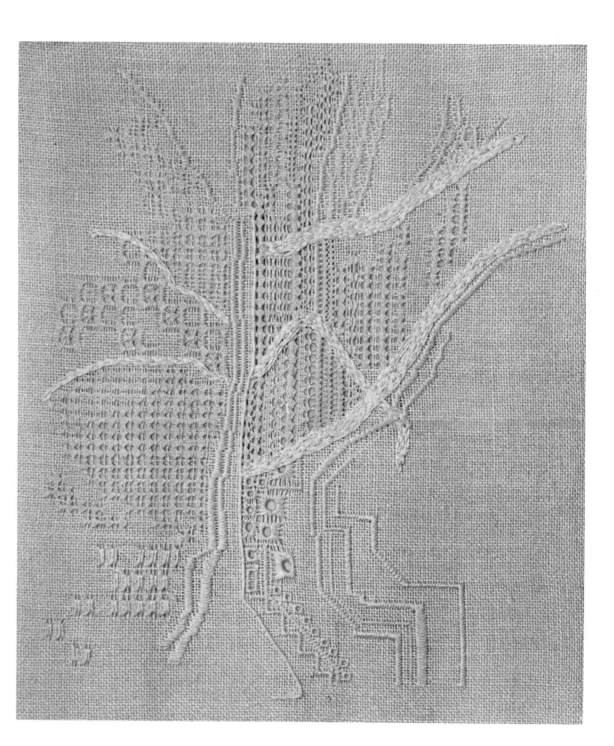

155 The delicate, lace-like texture of
a lichen (photograph by V A
Harding)

156 A lacy bed of bracken has a
texture which could be expressed in
fly stitch using a variety of threads in
several thicknesses (photograph by
J M Pickering)

157 *Far right* Patches of weed and
green algae float on the surface of
still waters like a patchwork of
machine embroidery (photograph by
R H Cuthbert)

Nature's Details

The study of nature's textures must inevitably lead us into a greater perception of detail in all its aspects. While we are examining the formation of a flower head we notice how its stamens are heart-shaped, or oval or divided into two, and that the arrangement of petals and stamens varies greatly from flower to flower. Look carefully at any vegetable you prepare for a meal and examine its structure, pattern, texture and colour. If possible, reserve one or two items for future study, then draw them, make prints with them, and use your research material as the basis for embroidery experiments to be used in the preparation of a larger-scale work.

Not only living plants reveal wonderful details, but dried and dead ones too have their own beauty. Pine cones, pineapple skins, dried prunes and fruit stones are all good study material. Unusually contorted pieces of wood can often be found when walking along the seashore; stripped of their bark, bleached by the sea and sun the linear patterns within each twist can be seen clearly, ready for immediate translation into couched threads or stitchery. Pick up other materials too, feathers, shells, pebbles, pieces of bark, dead insects; all these are valuable sources of design.

The benefits of detailed study will be even more fully appreciated when an embroidery is planned requiring exact information about eyes, feather formation, claws and feet, leaf joints, etc. Designs may be spoiled by insufficient observation of such details as the position of the wings on an insect or bird, the wrong kind of hoof on a mammal or the badly drawn joints of the legs. These things are important to the credibility of the design, even though it is often permissible to take small liberties along the way. Bad drawing, however, cannot be covered up by good technique, so time spent at this stage will be repayed.

Above and beyond the search for design is something far more long lasting. Developing at the same time will be an ability to *see* as an artist sees (as opposed to merely looking), a trained eye to note details which will be stored away for future use, the building up of information which, when manifested in drawings, often provokes 'non-observers' to wonder whether that information was given by divine right.

Detailed study takes place during every waking moment; it eventually becomes an unconscious act. It is not always necessary to see everything as embroidery, although the temptation may sometimes be so strong that it is impossible not to. Let the eye linger and probe, instead of flickering over what it sees; observe the colour of shadows and reflections, the shape of ripples on water. Observe all things, whether natural or manmade.

Do not put interesting things away in a safe drawer, leave them where you can see them at all times until you know them intimately, turning them over during a spare moment to rediscover what you saw in them previously. A gourd covered with grey, furry mould which at first you thought was weird or ugly may take on new dimensions, a new beauty even. Life will have become richer from that moment and your artistic awareness will have progressed that much more.

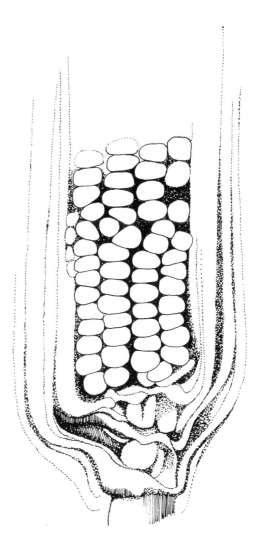

158 Corn on the cob

a

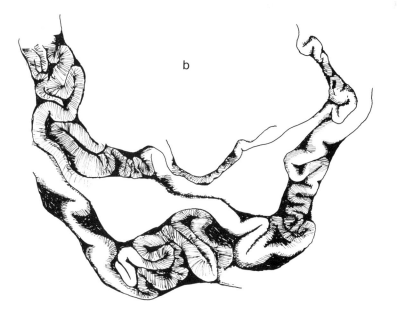

b

159 *Left* Frozen broccoli, a mixture
of larger shapes and rich texture
(photograph by V A Harding)

160 (a) Section of a cabbage
(photograph by V A Harding)
(b) Draw part of the crumpled
interior to find ideas for
manipulating fabric between areas of
high padding

161 Mushroom gill prints made on kitchen paper (photograph by V A Harding)

162 *Right* and *Above right*
Mushrooms and toadstools present a wide variety of forms; those which grow on trees are no less interesting than the free-standing ones. Note particularly the range of soft colours, the arrangement of gills, and the textures and patterns of the caps

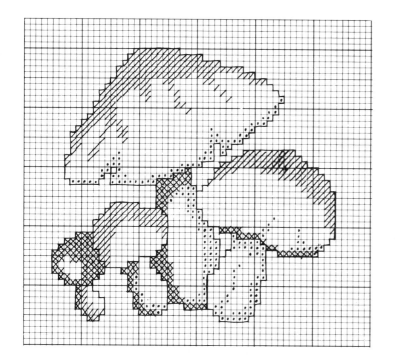

163 *Below* 'Mushrooms' by Freda Stoneman, embroidered on a printed fabric in rich browns and greens: the mushroom caps are of suede, slightly padded, with raised stitchery in wools and cottons (photograph by R H Cuthbert)

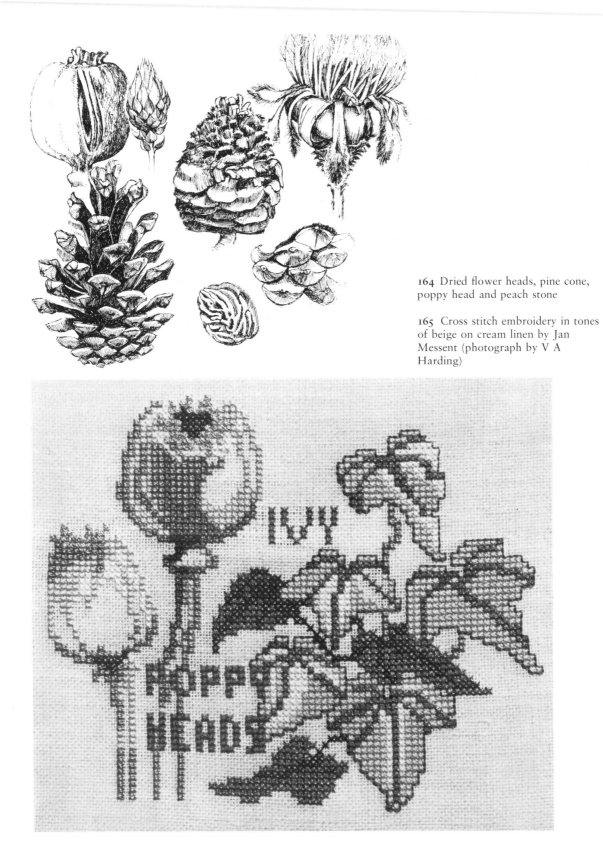

164 Dried flower heads, pine cone, poppy head and peach stone

165 Cross stitch embroidery in tones of beige on cream linen by Jan Messent (photograph by V A Harding)

166 The lid of a box, made by M Driver, based on the pattern of a pine cone, each small part being made separately and embroidered with gold and copper threads (photograph by R H Cuthbert)

167 Tiny flower heads of cow
parsley like dots of light arranged in
groups could be translated into
French knots and beads (photograph
by R H Cuthbert)

168 'Dahlia' by Anne Dyer, a study
in coloured felts of a dahlia head
showing the ingenious manipulation
of the fabric to achieve a three-
dimensional effect (photograph by
V A Harding)

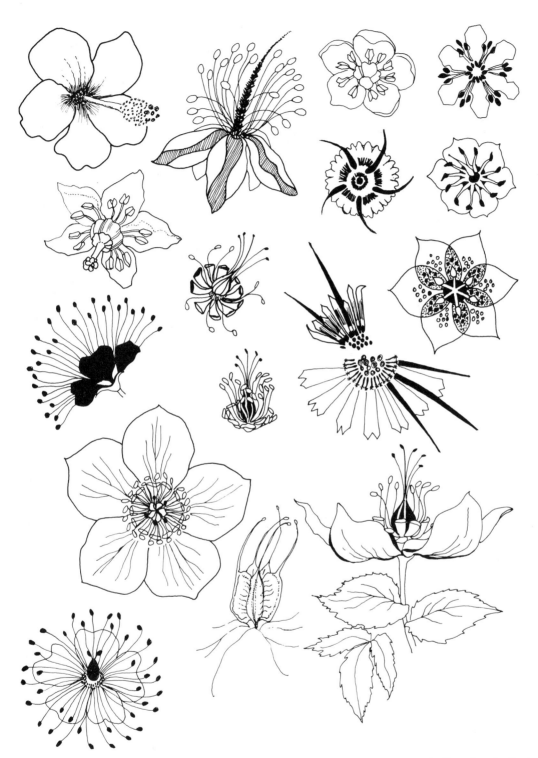

169 Drawings by Barbara Snook of flower heads showing many different arrangements of stamens and petals; observations of this kind are of great value to the embroiderer

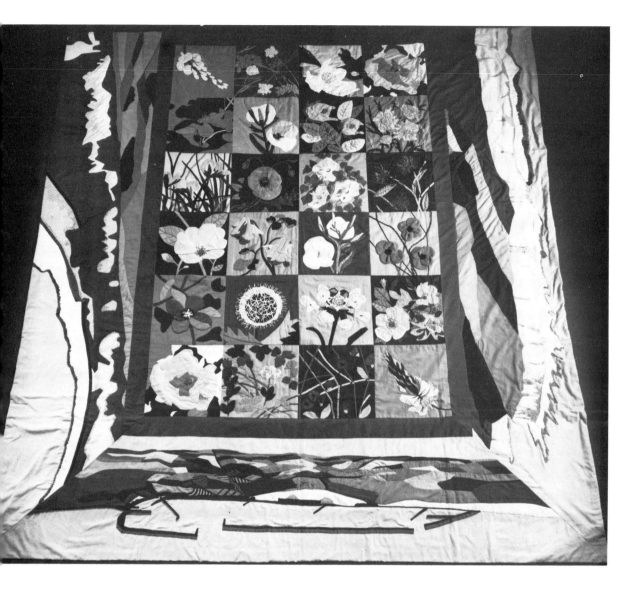

170 'The Dover Bedspread', designed by Ruth Issett and made by twenty-four members of the East Kent Embroiderers' Guild as a gift to the National Trust in 1976. It depicts the wild flowers which grow on the white cliffs of Dover, and each square of 30 cm (12 in) was worked separately in appliqué (photograph by Paul Simpson)

171 Pencil and paint sketch of freesias, by Judith Milne: the shape of the tube-like flower is clearly seen, with the right-angled bend of the stalk

172 Horse Chestnut bud opening (photograph by J M Pickering)

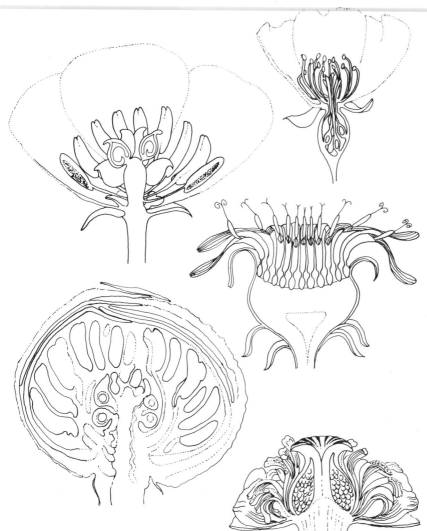

174 Sections of a rose, dandelion, buttercup and yellow water lily; biological supplier's catalogues and school text books are useful sources of drawings like this

175 *Opposite, above* Embroidery based on the vertical section of part of a flask fungus, worked in appliqué and stitchery (photograph by V A Harding)

176 (a) *Right* Head of a thistle (photograph by J M Pickering) (b) *Far right* Several Art Nouveau interpretations of the thistle head in a decorative style suitable for embroidery

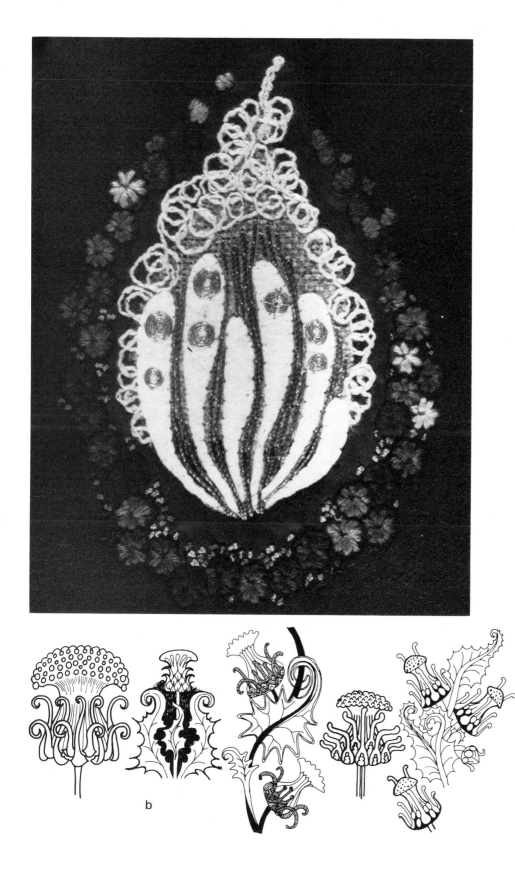

b

179 *Right* (a) 'Pebbles' by Jill Friend, showing the smooth, coloured lines often seen on pebbles, while others are encrusted with lichen and moss (photograph by R H Cuthbert)
(b) Detail of one of the pebbles by Jill Friend showing a mass of stitchery in the colours of moss and lichen (photograph by R H Cuthbert)

177 Plants with unusual shapes like the Wild Arum and the Horsetail make beautiful designs quite unlike any other

178 Grasses, drawn by Barbara Snook: delicate motifs like this need equally delicate treatments in embroidery

180 *Left* Driftwood on rocks: bleached and twisted wood provides a rich source of design material, to be taken home and studied in detail – wood grain and knots reveal flowing, rhythmic lines perfect for quilting designs (photograph by John Palmer)

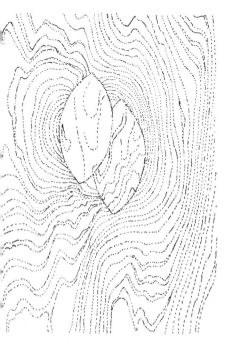

181 Wood grain and filled-up knot holes

182 A detail of 'Pine Bark' by Anne Dyer, a piece of three-dimensional canvaswork based on the part of a tree which had overgrown a sawn-off branch (photograph by V A Harding)

a

b

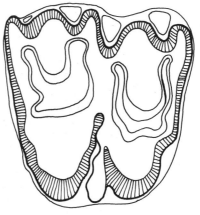

c

183 (a) Black ink drawing of a feather.
(b) The same design simplified and cut out of paper.
(c) The cut-paper design used for a piece of canvas embroidery by Jan Messent (photograph by V A Harding)

184 The fossil teeth of a herbivore

187 To make a symmetrical design, first draw half of it on tracing paper, fold this exactly down the centre and trace the other half; as long as the design on the two wings balances, there is no reason why they should be exactly alike in every detail

185 The details seen on butterflies' wings are well worth careful study; packets of wings may be bought from specialist shops, or observations may be made from good books

186 'Butterfly Quilt' by Marcia Learmouth measures 132 × 173 cm (52 × 68 in). The design was taken from about twenty drawings of butterflies' wings laid at random in a box. This produced a black and white design of patterns and textures which was then applied in fabrics of black, greys and soft muted shades which were seen in the pencil drawing (photograph by Millar and Harris)

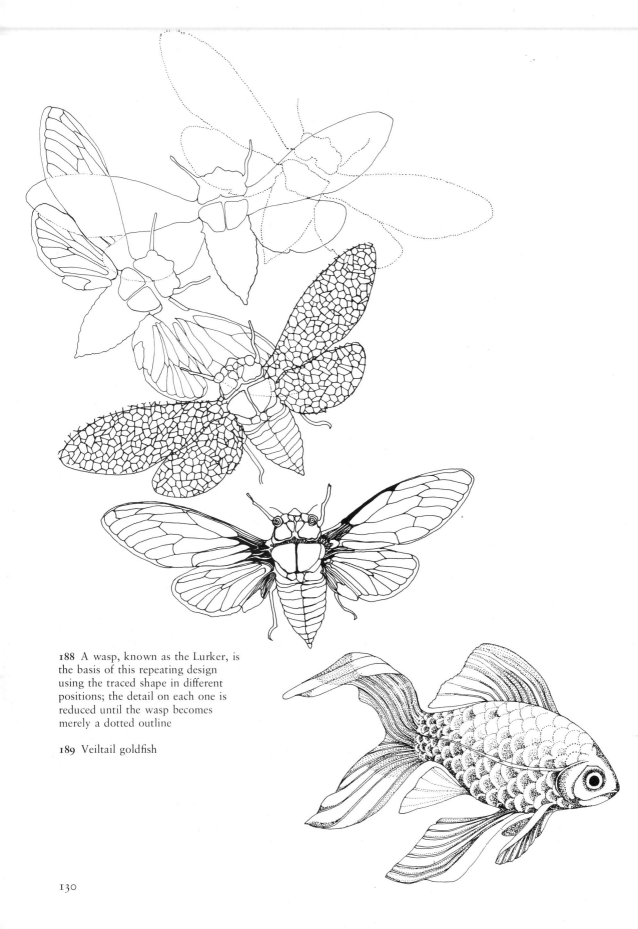

188 A wasp, known as the Lurker, is the basis of this repeating design using the traced shape in different positions; the detail on each one is reduced until the wasp becomes merely a dotted outline

189 Veiltail goldfish

190 Explore new ways of expressing details such as bird's eyes rather than using the well-worn cliché of a bead or a sequin. Study the expression of the eye during your research, draw it in several ways and try the methods shown here

a

b

191 (a) Beaks, claws and feathers are important details, too, which should be studied carefully during research. Although the arrangement of feathers is basically the same on all birds, the variations are caused by the different lengths and shapes, some of which are rounded and others pointed or squared off at the ends
(b) 'Golden Eagle' by Vera Bradshaw (photograph by R H Cuthbert)

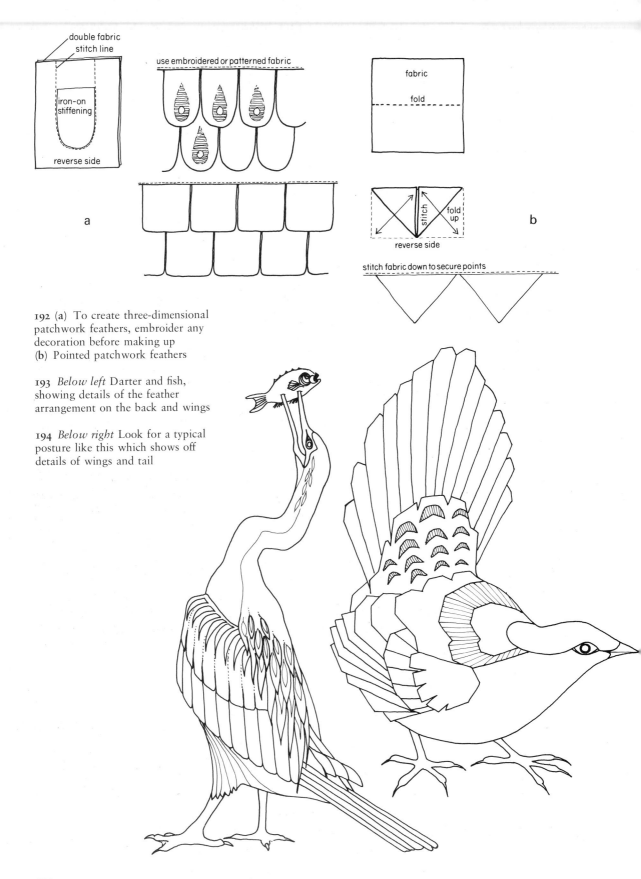

double fabric
stitch line

iron-on
stiffening

reverse side

use embroidered or patterned fabric

a

fabric

fold

stitch

fold up

reverse side

stitch fabric down to secure points

b

192 (a) To create three-dimensional
patchwork feathers, embroider any
decoration before making up
(b) Pointed patchwork feathers

193 *Below left* Darter and fish,
showing details of the feather
arrangement on the back and wings

194 *Below right* Look for a typical
posture like this which shows off
details of wings and tail

195 *Left* Horns add greatly to the decorative value of an animal – the striations, ridges and twists show the direction which stitches might take, both across the horn and along it

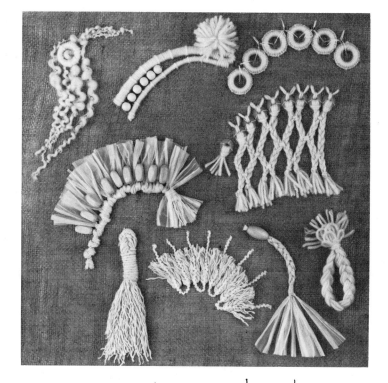

196 For manes and tails, the design and materials should relate to those used on the rest of the animal; the examples shown are made from plaited wools and raffia with beads, washers and rings, and threads pulled from the background fabric (photograph by Gail Bathgate)

197 *Right* Animals' feet vary considerably in shape and are an important detail which should be noted when making preliminary drawings: (*left to right*) horse, antelope, bull, lion, camel, (*top right*) elephant, bear

Nature at a Distance

Panoramic views may be seen by some embroiderers as an irresistible challenge but there are many others to whom the size and complexity of an outdoor scene may prove too daunting to inspire them to embroider it. Those in the latter group are advised that there are ways round these problems. The first one is to go slowly, not to rush immediately into an embroidery, but to sit and look at the scene for as long as possible to absorb the colours, tones, shapes and textures, and to disregard those parts which have no relevance.

One way to eliminate extraneous parts of a scene is to use a frame of card or paper as a window through which you look to capture a view inside. Move it about over the scene to find a pleasing arrangement of tones and shapes then sketch your framed view in a rectangle of the same shape. Make several sketches, if necessary, with notes of colours and textures, then make more detailed sketches, without the frame, of parts nearer to you.

This idea may be taken one step further by making the window part of the finished design. Instead of simply a rectangle, cut out a window frame of several sections, either small panes or larger arches (see figure 214), and see your view through this, incorporating the window frame into your embroidery.

Successful designs of outdoor scenes can often be made from photographs, though one should beware of the too brilliant colours seen on some postcards. Remember that colours tend to lose their brilliance the further away we are from them.

The study of landscape painters may sometimes help to crystallise one's thoughts on the subject, especially the following:

Rousseau: stylized and darkly mystical
Van Gogh: turbulence and richly-coloured landscapes
Seurat: pointillism – tiny dots of colour blending together
Manet: soft, delicate and misty colours
Maurice Denis: lovely 'machine embroidery' textures
Jacques Villon: cubism – soft, pastel patchworks of colour.

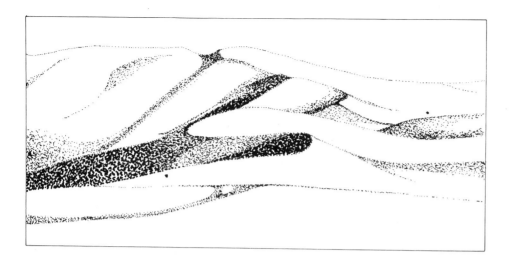

198 The rhythmic lines of sand dunes could be translated into French knots and seeding, machine embroidery or quilting

199 Aerial photographs of land often reveal patterns of rhythmic lines perfect for embroidery: this one shows cultivated land which could provide a design for goldwork, couching or quilting

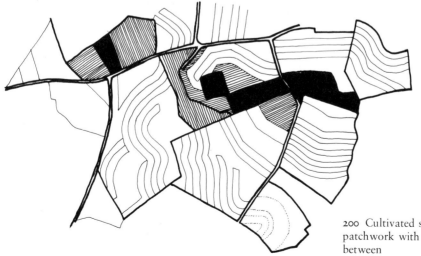

200 Cultivated strips of land form a patchwork with roads and forests between

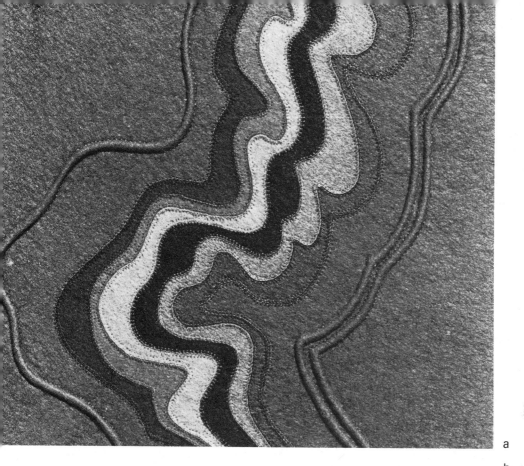

a

b

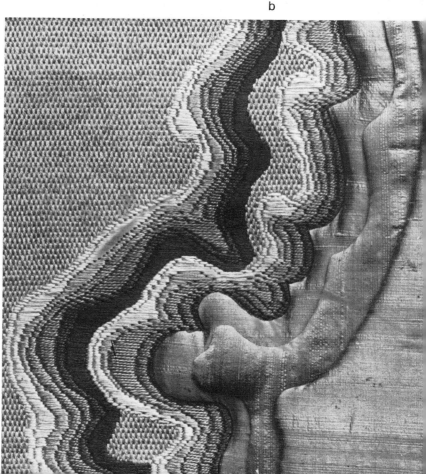

201 *Facing page* 'Garden Cushion' by Jean Curran: strips of brown corduroy sewn together in different directions catch the light like cultivated soil – ruched velvet and thickly embroidered wool suggest brilliant foliage which spills over onto the other side (photograph by R H Cuthbert)

202 The contorted moraines of a glacier show swirling lines of great beauty (photograph by Bradford Washburn)

203 (a) 'Linear Design I' by Heide Jenkins, a design inspired by an aerial view of a shoreline, worked in felt inlay with corded quilting (photograph by V A Harding) (b) 'Linear Design II' by Heide Jenkins uses the same design, worked this time in padded silk and canvas embroidery; the smoothness of the silk makes an excellent foil for the busier texture of the stitchery (photograph by V A Harding)

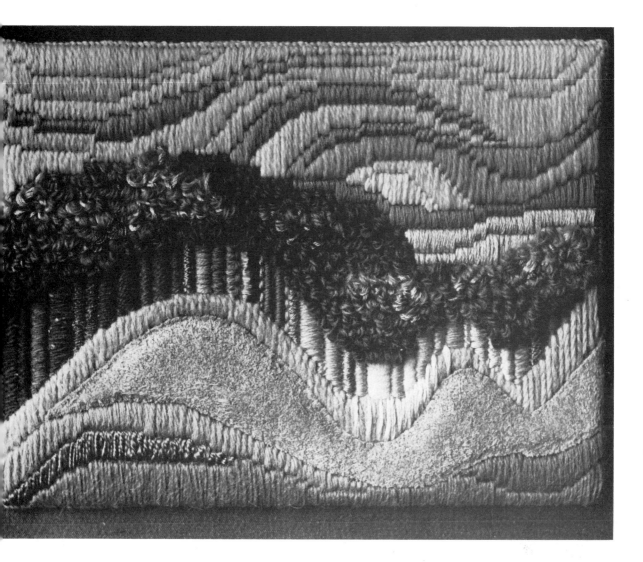

204 *Left above* Snow, sunlight, cloud, swirling lines and shadows make an arrangement of tones perfect for blackwork, goldwork or quilting (photograph by Bradford Washburn)

205 *Left* 'My North Country' by Jan Messent, worked on coarse scrim, with medical gauze and Vilene, needleweaving, pulled work and limpet shells: an attempt to capture the stark beauty of the Yorkshire Dales, the limestone scree slithering down from the fells and the snow still 'on the tops' (photograph by V A Harding)

206 Small canvaswork panel by Jan Messent illustrating how straight stitches can be used to express curves; the small area of padded suede provides a relief from the highly textured areas (photograph by Norman Weston)

207 (a) Drawing by Muriel Best of a bunch of dried Sycamore keys; no shading is shown, only the outlines. It was noticed that, turned on its side, the drawing resembled a landscape

(b) Tracing paper was laid over the drawing which was then re-traced, leaving out some details and simplifying others to make it look even more like fields and trees

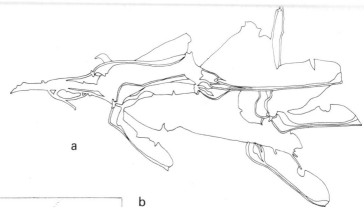

a

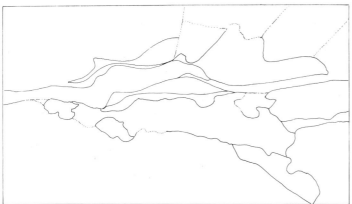

b

(c) 'Summer Landscape' by Muriel Best, designed from the simplified drawings of Sycamore keys. The use of straight stitches, French knots, fly and sorbello stitches with the successful distribution of tonal areas lends charm to this 'accidental' design (photograph by V A Harding)

208 'Striped Field II', an experimental sketch by Charis Weller, based on a photograph by Richard Summersby. Worked on off-white cotton, the fabric was coloured with felt-tipped pens and pencils, then made wet so that the colours blurred and mixed. Terylene wadding was then placed beneath, and the design was machined freely on top with sewing cotton (photograph by V A Harding)

209 'Paysage' by Jenny Bullen, white cotton, wetted, then dabbed with dye-powder after first quilting the main outlines; more quilting was added later (photograph by V A Harding)

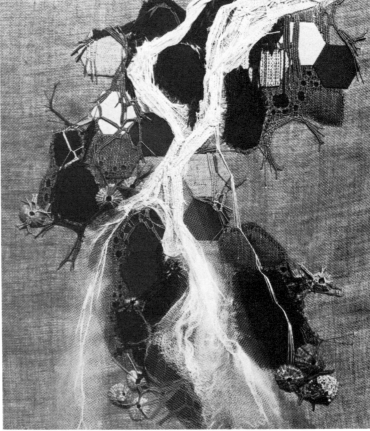

210 'Cornish Waves' by Christine Andrews, a seascape inspired by crashing waves under a windswept sky: the texture of sea and rocks is well expressed in the use of ruched fabrics and furry threads (photograph by R H Cuthbert)

211 'My North Country II' by Jan Messent, needleweaving and patchwork on coarse scrim over medical gauze and net, with limpet shells and padding (photograph by V A Harding)

212 *Left* Part of the water gardens at Clivedon Manor, Buckinghamshire (photograph by R H Cuthbert)

213 *Right* The effect of distance is achieved by allowing the colours in the distance to lose their intensity while those in the foreground become gradually stronger, deeper and more precise in detail (photograph by R H Cuthbert)

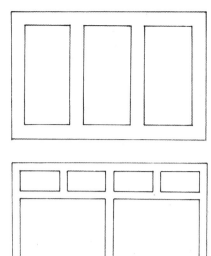

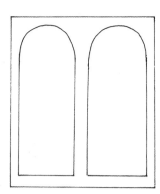

214 Window shapes may become part of the embroidery

215 (a) 'Kitchen Window' by Valerie Harding shows a door of quilted calico through which can be seen a section of garden worked in straight stitches (photograph by V A Harding)

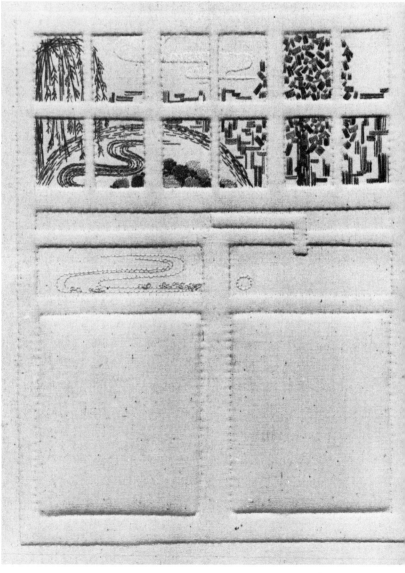

(b) 'Elizabethan Garden' by Audrey Ormrod is embroidered entirely in cross stitch on a fairly coarse linen, using stranded cottons and some heavier threads on the darker foliage. The use of cross stitch is most effective in this interpretation of a formal garden, with its regular pattern of flower beds, trimmed hedges and walls

216 *Top* Animals seen from a distance often make silhouettes against a pale background; this idea could be used to concentrate all the detail on the scenery while keeping the animal shapes completely plain

217 *Centre* Stark tree-tops against the sky make a dramatic design for stitchery or needleweaving

218 *Below* A pattern of penguins seen from a distance against the snow shows only the darker parts of the birds

219 (a) *Above right* A sunlit landscape seen from the deep shadow of woodland makes a dramatic contrast of tones; changes of texture can also be seen in the roughness of the foreground and the shaven fields beyond (photograph by R H Cuthbert)
(b) *Below right* 'Trees' by Christine Andrews creates a similar impression of contrasts by needleweaving on several layers in front of a soft, light background of smooth fabrics (photograph by R H Cuthbert)

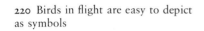

220 Birds in flight are easy to depict as symbols

221 Seen at a distance, different kinds of birds are recognisable by their dimensions and form

222 Pencil and paint sketch by Sarah Harding of fighting birds: although no details can be seen, the aggressive position of the beating wings immediately suggests tension and fast movement (photograph by V A Harding)

Nature in Three Dimensions

Though embroidery is generally regarded as a two-dimensional art, investigations into its history will show that constant explorations have been made throughout the centuries to create an impression of volume and high relief finally resulting in completely free-standing embroideries.

In making a three-dimensional embroidery the construction and final making up must play a very important part in producing a balanced and structurally sound piece of work. It is sometimes necessary to make a 'mock up' first in order to find out what difficulties in construction lie ahead, and to make the pattern pieces for use on the real thing. Much unnecessary disappointment can be avoided in this way.

Every fabric has its own characteristic behaviour when laid flat and when used three-dimensionally, and constant experimentation is essential to discover the potential of all kinds of fabrics. Canvas is stiff and holds its shape well but frays round the edges unless these are glued before covering with thread. Velvet has a nap which will take on new tones when held in different directions; stripes will appear curved when sewn over bumps (see figure 223). Leather can be difficult to sew or may tear; curved card needs a bias-cut fabric to cover it – all these and many more details should be investigated at a preliminary stage as no drawing, however detailed, will supply this information.

Embroidered toys can be made, if desired, by using a commercial pattern of a suitable nature and embroidering on the fabric *before* cutting out. This will allow for any contraction of the fabric made by the stitches pulling the fibres closer together. Simply tack round the pattern pieces to indicate the shapes, and when the embroidery is completed, lay the pattern pieces on the fabric *again* to check that the shapes are still the same. Make any necessary adjustments before cutting out, sewing up and stuffing.

Simple shapes can sometimes be used as cushions, and these may be painted with fabric dye before being embroidered or quilted. See the chapter on 'Textures' for some ways of achieving a high relief effect, and let the ideas from nature stimulate further attempts to experiment with free-form quilting, canvaswork, padded patchwork, pulled thread, appliqué, wrapped wire and threads, tubes of fabric and fabric-covered card shapes. Look for small, simple shapes to begin with, leaves, limpets, flower-heads, butterflies, simple insects and birds, before moving on to the more complex ones.

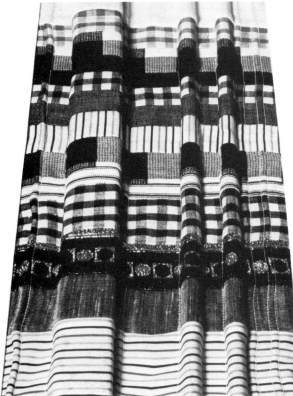

223 Striped and checked fabric shows marked changes when sewn over ridges and bumps (photograph by David Prout)

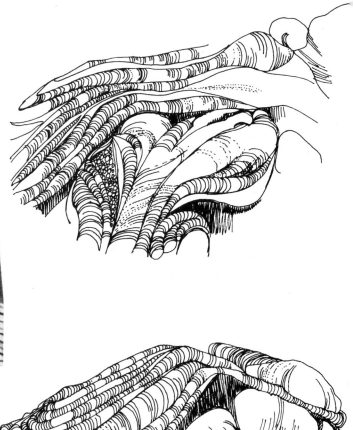

224 Sketches of laval forms by Judith Milne

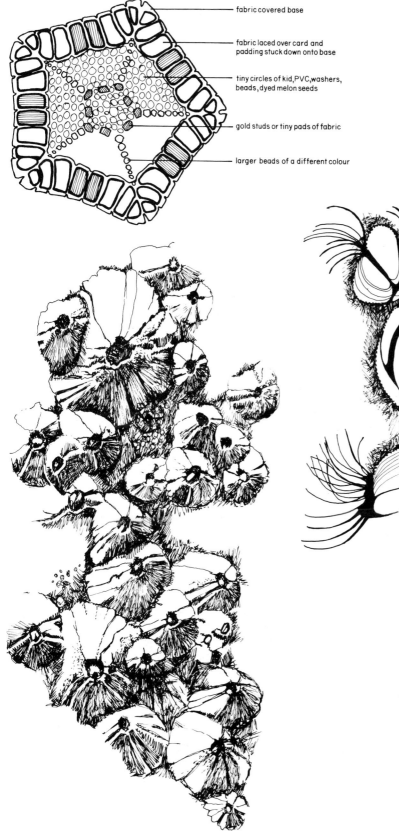

fabric covered base

fabric laced over card and padding stuck down onto base

tiny circles of kid, PVC, washers, beads, dyed melon seeds

gold studs or tiny pads of fabric

larger beads of a different colour

225 A starfish motif could be used for a box-top, a three-dimensional panel or a cushion

226 *Above* Goose barnacles

227 *Left* Acorn barnacles can be translated into three-dimensional embroidery by the use of padded cones of fabric or kid, or circles of fabric gathered tightly at the centre, padded, and sewn into creases round the edges

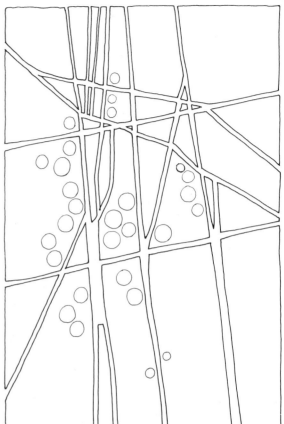

228 (a) *Above* Pen and ink drawing on textured Letraset paper of limpets between cracks of rocks

(b) *Above right* The drawing can be simplified by tracing and slightly rearranging the lines to create a design for padded shapes and jewelled cones in high relief

229 (a) *Left* A contrast of textures
seen in the dried bank of the river
reflected in dark water with the round
smoothness of stones on the edge
(photograph by R H Cuthbert)
(b) *Above* 'Reflections' by Penelope
Cuthbert, translated as a mirror
surrounded by the colours and
textures of earth and leaves in three
dimensions (photograph by
R H Cuthbert)
(c) *Above right* Detail of
'Reflections' by Penelope Cuthbert,
showing the padded suede and satiny
pebbles, with shiny stones and French
knots (photograph by R H Cuthbert)

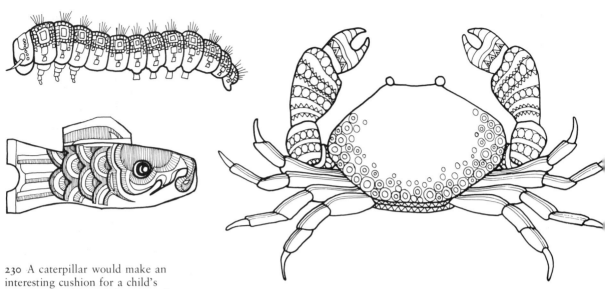

230 A caterpillar would make an interesting cushion for a child's room, as would a fish based on the design of Oriental paper toys

231 Decorative crab

232 *Left* 'Pink Crab' by Joan
Thatcher, and 'Starfish Box' by Jan
Messent: the crab is completely three-
dimensional, made of pink felt and
richly embroidered, and the box was
made to resemble a striped boulder
topped by a pink silk starfish on
crocheted seaweed (photograph by
Norman Weston)

233 Jewelled fish in a basket
would make an interesting three-
dimensional embroidery

234 Fossil sea-lily, a member of
the animal family (courtesy of the
British Museum, Natural History)

235 'Hanging Onions' by Mary Shea: the papery quality of the skins is suggested by pulled fabric, netting, machine quilting and stitching, with wrapped threads (photograph by R H Cuthbert)

236 'Strawberries' by Heide Jenkins, made of red, pink and white satin embroidered with seeding stitches. The leaves are stiffened on the underside with suede and are attached to stems of wrapped wire, each one quilted to suggest veins (photograph by R H Cuthbert)

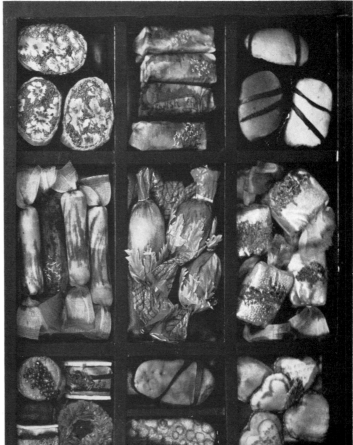

237 *Above* A tangle of old roots and branches lying among the reflections of its neighbouring trees is the kind of three-dimensional shape one can see when out walking; notice the plants growing on and around it and the contrast of the delicate grasses (photograph by R H Cuthbert)

238 'Garden Assortment' by Millie Stevens – a wooden box is divided into compartments which are filled with embroidered sweets resembling 'things from the garden'. All are in green-yellow colours, some wrapped in leafy-green paper and some in painted chiffon and gauze (photograph by Norman Weston)

239 'Hanging Basket' by Valerie
Harding: canvaswork plants, each
one made separately and attached by
means of wrapped wire stalks to a
wire basket shape – brilliant greens,
reds and pinks are the colours used
(photograph by V A Harding)

240 'Ivy Mirror' by Charis Weller, a design inspired by seeing variegated ivy growing up a wall. Each leaf is worked separately on canvas and wired along the veins; the background is a mixture of canvaswork and applied suede, with the mirror inset behind (photograph by V A Harding)

241 A pencil study of amaryllis by Judith Milne, showing the construction of the flower, its markings, the position and number of the stamens and the form of the petals. A study of this kind is invaluable when beginning a three-dimensional embroidery, as the construction is all-important

242 *Right* 'Wedding Bouquet' by Valerie Williams, based on the bouquet which she carried at her own wedding: white satin machine-edged flowers with machine embroidered shading inside, and dark green velvet leaves, wired to keep their shape (photograph by V A Harding)

243 (a) *Left* A hedgerow, prickly and defensive from the outside, harbours dark secrets within (photograph by Jean Littlejohn)

(b) *Below* 'Play Hedge for Hannah' by Jean Littlejohn captures the mystery of a thick hedge in this three-dimensional construction; deep inside can be seen a bird in its nest, a tiny dormouse and a hedgehog (photograph by R H Cuthbert)

244 A shire horse marked into areas where padding would correctly be placed to suggest the contours of the body

245 'Camel' by Jan Messent, appliqué with three-dimensional packs attached. This could provide ideas for a school class project, each child being able to contribute some detail by making the pompoms and fringes or sewing on the 'contraband' amber beads under one of the bags (photograph by David Prout)

246 'Armadillo' by Valerie Harding.
A superb example of good
construction, this delightful creature
is covered with brown leather and
gold and green leather pieces; studs
and beads are attached to form a rich
pattern (photograph by V A
Harding)

Bibliography

History of Embroidery

LUBELL, Cecil (editor) *Textile Collections of the World Vols I & II*, Studio Vista, London, 1976

SNOOK, Barbara *English Embroidery* Batsford, London, 1970; Mills and Boon, London 1974.

General embroidery

JONES, Nora *Embroidery* (Guidlines Series) Macdonald Educational, 1978

PYMAN, Kit *Needle Craft Series, Nos 1–16* Search Press, London, 1979

PHILLPOTT, Pat *The Craft of Embroidery* Stanley Paul, London, 1976

WHYTE, Kathleen *Design in Embroidery* Batsford, London, 1969

Plant life

HART, Cyril & RAYMOND, Charles *British Trees in Colour* Book Club Associates (Rainbird), London, 1973

LEHANE, Brendan *The Power of Plants* John Murray, London, 1977

NILSSON, PERSSON & MOSSBERG *Fungi, Vols I & II* Penguin (Nature Guides), 1978

NICHOLSON & BRIGHTMAN *The Oxford Book of Flowerless Plants* Oxford University Press, 1979

Animal life

WILWERDING, Walter J *Animal Drawing and Painting* Dover, New York, 1966

Birds

BRUUN, Bertel *Guide to Birds of Britain and Europe* Hamlyn, London, 1974

LLOYD, Glenys & Derek *Birds of Prey* Hamlyn, London, 1975

The World Atlas of Birds, Mitchell Beazley, London, 1974

Insects

SEGUY, E A *Decorative Butterflies and Insects*, Dover, New York, 1977

The sea

ABBOTT, R Tucker *Seashells*, Bantam/Ridge Press, New York, 1976

MARSHALL, Norman & Olga *Ocean Life*, Blandford Press, London, 1971

Minerals and rocks

KOURIMSKY, Dr J K *Illustrated Encyclopedia of Minerals and Rocks*, Octopus, London, 1977

Microscopic life

Images From Life, British Museum, London 1971

General

Joy of Nature, Reader's Digest, 1978

Suppliers

Great Britain

Mary Allen	Wirksworth, Derbyshire DE4 4BN
Brodwaith Embroidery	5 Lion Yard, Dolgellau, Gwynedd
Cotswold Craft Centre	(mail order only), Mrs R Tyley, 5 Whitehall, Stroud, Gloucestershire GL5 1HA
Campden Needlework Centre	High Street, Chipping Campden, Gloucestershire
de Denne Ltd	159–161 Kenton Road, Kenton, Harrow, Middlesex
Ruth John (callers by appointment)	39 The Square, Titchfield, Hampshire, PO14 4AP
Mace and Nairn	89 Crane Street, Salisbury, Wiltshire
Christine Riley	53 Barclay Street, Stonehaven, Kincardineshire
Silken Strands (mail order)	33 Linksway, Gatley, Cheadle, Cheshire SK8 4LA
Texere Yarns	9 Peckover Street, Bradford, West Yorkshire BD1 5BD
The Felt and Hessian Shop (B Brown Ltd)	32–33 Greville Street, London EC1
The Handicraft Shop	5 Oxford Road, Altrincham, Cheshire WA14 2DY

USA

Appleton Brothers of London	West Main Road, Little Compton, Rhode Island 02837
American Crewel Studio	Box 298, Boonton, New Jersey 07005
American Thread Corporation	90 Park Avenue, New York
Bucky King Embroideries Unlimited	Box 371, King Bros, 3 Ranch Buffalo Star Rte, Sheriden, Wyoming 82801
Casa de las Tejedoras	1618 East Edinger, Santa Ana, California 94704
Craft Kaleidoscope	6412 Ferguson Street, Indianapolis 46220
Dharma Trading Company	1952 University Avenue, Berkeley, California 94704
Folklorico Yarn Co	522 Ramona Street, Palo Alto, California 94301
The Golden Eye	Box 205, Chestnut Hill, Massachusetts 02167
Heads and Tails	River Forest, Illinois 60305
Lily Mills	Shelby, North Carolina 28150
Threadbenders	2260 Como Avenue, St Paul, Minnesota 55108
The Thread Shed	307 Freeport Road, Pittsburgh, Pennsylvania 15215
Yarn Depot	545 Sutter Street, San Francisco, California 94118

Canada

Sutton Yarns	2054 Yonge Street, Toronto, Ontario
Leonida Leatherdale Embroidery Studio	90 East Gate, Winnipeg, Manitoba R3C 2C3

Index